The Guide to JAPANESE FOOD AND RESTAURANTS

by
Russell Marcus
Jack Plimpton

D0172927

SHUFUNOTOMO CO., LTD

Photographs
Cover and P.160: Inakaya, Akasaka
P.132: Kushinobo, Ginza
P.156: Benihana of New York, Ginza
P.162: Nanbantei, Shibuya
P.168: Chotoku, Shibuya
(Photos by Takehiko Takei)
P.166: Katsushin, Ueno (Photo by Keiichi Kato)

Recipe
P.159: Kazunari Yanagihara

First printing, 1984

Published by Shufunotomo Co., Ltd.
6, Kanda Surugadai 1-chome,
Chiyoda-ku, Tokyo,
Japan 101

Printed in Japan

ISBN4-07-974015-8

PREFACE

This is the travel guide to Japanese cuisine that tourists, businessmen and gourmets have been waiting for.

Imagine trying to find a Barbecued Chicken Pub or a *Kaiseki* Haute Cuisine Restaurant on your own in Tokyo! This Guide makes it possible. It tells you what restaurants look like from the outside, and exactly where they are in the city. Detailed street and subway maps together with English-language landmarks steer you to 740 restaurants. The maps by themselves are worth the price of the book.

More importantly, this guidebook tells you what to expect when you get inside—about the decor and atmosphere, and about those little skewers of barbecued chicken and vegetables you're hunting for. Bilingual menus and phrases simplify the task of ordering. With the GOURMET TIPS sections you can become a true connoisseur of Japanese cuisines!

In Japan, restaurants are devoted to one of eighteen specialty cuisines. Specialization—be it in the art of preparing *tempura*, *sushi* or pork cutlets—leads to perfection. Now, thanks to the Guide's easy-to-use RESTAURANT FINDER and thumb tabs, even the novice can choose the food perfect for his or her own mood and palate.

The 740 recommended restaurants are culled from over 45,000 in the Tokyo area. In selecting them, we relied on our own gustatory explorations, the assembled knowledge of three dozen Japanese gourmet guidebooks, and a careful consideration of the restaurants' location and accessibility to foreigners. We believe that our selections capture the rich diversity of Japan's cuisines, restaurant decors, and price ranges. The Guide is thoroughly cross indexed by type of cuisine, section of town, and restaurant name to assist the diner in finding a suitable restaurant fast.

A final caveat—Japanese prefer restaurants that are cozy and very rich in Japanese culture. We urge you to read the introduction carefully in order to fully enjoy what is, for the westerner, a very exotic dining experience. The Guide contains much useful information which will allow you to get the most out of Japan. We mean it when we wish you, *"Bon Appetit!"*

The authors doing research for this Guide.

ACKNOWLEDGEMENTS

The authors would like to extend their sincere thanks to many persons and individuals who helped in the project to bring this Guide into being.

In particular, we wish to thank Ajinomoto Co. Inc. for providing access to one of the world's largest libraries on Japanese foods in its Center for Dietary Culture, and the Japanese Chefs Association for introducing the many culinary experts we interviewed. We also want to thank Messrs. Aoyama Torinosuke, Masaaki Oghi and especially *Kaichi* Tsuji, fourth in a line of *kaiseki* master chefs, for their valuable gourmet information.

In addition, we would like to acknowledge the assistance of Messrs. D.A. Shepardson, Yoshikazu Itoh, Han Morinaga, Sumiko Konami and of course the following supervisors and researchers whose survey work was used in this Guide:

—Supervisors: Sago Rie and Yoshii Tohru

—Researchers: Abe Hirohiko, Abe Yoshimi, Hori Tetsuhiko, Kamibayashi Satoru, Koga Yuko, Minai Masahiko, Nakanishi Fujio, Ogiwara Sozo, Saiki Toneo, Sawafuji Hiroko, Shigematsu Hiroshi, Shindo Makiko, Tsuruta Ikuko, Wada Kuniaki and Yamase Hiroshi and Elon Simon.

We note with special thanks the computer assistance received from Dr. S.J. Bellamy, P.W. Laney, R. May, P. Perkins, J. Davis, R.A. Simon, D.W. Hayman and A.L. Ham. And finally, we wish to express our sincere appreciation for all the effort and cooperation extended to us by the staff at Shufunotomo to turn our manuscript into a wonderful gourmet Guide.

CONTENTS

Casseroles and Stews

Deep-Fried Specialties

Noodles and Do-It-Yourself Pizza

● Dining Maps

● Appendices

● Indexes

INTRODUCTION AND GENERAL TIPS

The Japanese Restaurant Mystique

When the present Japanese Emperor gave his daughter, Princess Takako, to be married, the engagement ceremony was held in a Japanese restaurant. No ordinary restaurant to be sure, but this fact tells us something about the distinctive character of restaurants in Japan. The atmosphere and setting of Japanese restaurants is a cultural nexus for the Japanese. Even when they are located in the heart of a city, Japanese restaurants are sanctuaries, microcosms with attentive service and an ambience reminiscent of a time when the Shoguns ruled.

To the hungry tourist or businessman, Japanese restaurants provide a hearty feast of the most decorative, freshest vittles on earth. But the adventure-hungry will find more: an older Japan, a land shed of its Western modernity, full of the grace, mystique and yes, the Japanese spirit whose flames the hearth has kept alive and exciting.

Tokyo is Japan's Restaurant Capital

Tokyo, Japan's dining capital, has more than 45,000 Japanese restaurants from which to choose. If you were to sample all of them, it would take 123 years! The reason for so many restaurants is to serve zealous Tokyoites who spend twice as much per person in restaurants than do Japanese from any other region. On a single block alone, there may be 10 restaurants crowded together all jockeying for customers. Such is the dining potential of Tokyo.

Features of the Guide

The Guide to Japanese Food and Restaurants tells you just about everything you need to know to dine at a Japanese restaurant with ease. It is the first guidebook in English to unlock the language and culture barriers so as to make dining Japanese style a fun and delicious experience.

1. Restaurant Finding Features

RESTAURANT FINDER (inside the front cover) tells where to find Japanese specialty restaurants and cuisines in Tokyo by indicating the concentration of recommended restaurants for each cuisine in each of Tokyo's 10 restaurant centers.

RECOMMENDED RESTAURANTS (a section at the end of every chapter) tells where to find the best restaurants in Tokyo for every specialty and cuisine. Stars identify the most highly recommended throughout the Guide. **Example**, ☆ 3–7 means that you should use MAP 3 and look on it for restaurant No. 7 which is a highly recommended restaurant.

MAPS of the restaurants centers tell where to find the nearest restaurants in Tokyo and identify over 700 recommended restaurants, with symbols indicating each restaurant's specialty or cuisine.

CUISINE TABS show which maps contain the type of specialty restaurant or cuisine are on each map page.

INDEX TO RESTAURANT NAMES (see page 257) let's you look up good restaurants you've heard about.

RECOGNIZING THE RESTAURANT and restaurant ATMOSPHERE AND SERVICE (sections and features of most chapters) tell you how to tell a restaurant from a bathhouse, and what clues to look for to identify what kind of food the restaurant serves. The code restaurants use to identify their cuisine is summarized on page 11.

2. Food Information Features

Chapters provide fascinating descriptions of the 18 major types of Japanese cuisines, and also tell what makes a particular style of cooking a treat. In other words, everything you always wanted to know about Japanese food, but didn't know how to ask a Japanese chef.

GOURMET TIPS (a section and feature of most chapters) explains what the Japanese prize in a certain type of cuisine and gives you intimate facts about Japanese foods you can use to impress your friends and associates with.

RESTAURANT FINDER (inside front cover) lists page number references to both information about Japanese cuisines (what to eat) and to the maps of Tokyo's restaurant centers (where to dine). The RESTAURANT FINDER also indicates the prices and styles of dining service.

3. Menu Ordering Features

ORDERING FROM THE MENU (a section in most chapters) describes standard menu and typical dishes which you can order when you find the menu is written entirely in Japanese.

USEFUL PHRASES FOR ORDERING (see page 21) permits you to speak in Japanese about dining essentials.

GLOSSARY OF JAPANESE FOOD WORDS (see page 251) is a reference tool to ensure you can get the foods you want.

KANA ALPHABET FINDER (see page 25) is a language tool for reading the names of dishes which are often written is *kana* characters. This Guide also presents a system for learning to read *kanji* numbers (see page 24).

LIST OF JAPANESE FISH AND SEAFOOD NAMES (see page 75) enables you to decipher the numerous Japanese fish and seafood names.

4. Street Navigation Features

Detailed MAPS designed for your convenience show only the English signs on a street. In other words, you'll find all names on the MAPS in English on actual building signs. If you don't read Japanese, these MAPS are a fantastic asset to figure out where you are and how to get to a destination without getting lost, and without having to ask passerbys for directions.

Subway exit numbers are included for first time in an English language guidebook so that you can know which subway exit will bring you nearest to your destination. This Guide also gives you a simple way to read and remember the *kanji* characters on station exit signs (see page 18).

The 18 Major Types of Japanese Specialty Restaurants

In the West, we choose a cuisine by country: French sauces and viandes, Italian pasta, etc. In Japan, each style of cooking has a specialty restaurant unto itself, from dunking to frying, grilling, slicing, simmering and broiling. (The restaurants associated with these specific techniques are: *tonkatsu*, *teppanyaki*, *robatayaki*, *sashimi*, *oden* and *yakitori*, to name a few.) In all of them, cooking techniques have been refined and perfected. At *tempura* restaurants, for example, the art of deep-frying is so developed, that chefs can fry ice cream and accurately measure the temperature of boiling oil by feeling the pressure it exerts on a chopstick!

Ingredients as well as techniques form the basis for a distinctive specialty restaurant. Pork is served at *ton-*

katsu-ya (the *ya* means restaurant), eel at *unagi-ya*, chicken at *yakitori-ya*, beef at *sukiyaki* and *teppanyaki* restaurants, and fish, well, fish is served at many restaurants. Always, the tendency to specialize and to perfect service and techniques is rampant.

In total, there are 18 major types of Japanese specialty restaurants. Although you probably are acquainted with *sushi*, *tempura* and *sukiyaki*, Japanese restaurants have many other specialties: seasonal delicacies, beef, chicken, pork, seafood, grilled specialties, deep-fried meals, casseroles and stews, and inexpensive dishes such as "do-it-yourself pizza" and noodles. Each type of restaurant and the speciality it offers is described in a separate **CHAPTER**, classified by eight cuisine categories in the order shown below.

General Restaurants
1. **Regional Specialty Houses**: *Kyodo-ryori*, regional specialties.
2. **General Restaurants**: *Nihon-ryori*, a variety of Japanese cuisines served at a single restaurant. Other names for such general restaurants are *wafu* and *washoku* (literally, "Japanese style", "Japanese cuisine"), and *kisetsu-ryori* (literally, "seasonal" specialties).

Seasonal Restaurants
3. **Japanese Haute Cuisine**: *Kaiseki*, traditional courses of exquisitely prepared dishes. A variation of *kaiseki* from Kyoto is *Kyo-ryori*:
4. **Cordon Bleu Restaurants**: *Kappo*, customer-requested specialties prepared by a master chef.

Beef
5. **Beef Saute/Fondu Restaurants**: *Sukiyaki*, pan simmered beef and vegetables. Usually available with

delectable *shabu-shabu*, thinly sliced and parboiled beef.

6. **Steak Grills**: *Teppanyaki*, steak, seafood, vegetables and noodles grilled on a giant tableside griddle iron.

Seafood

7. **Fresh Seafood Cuisines**: *Sushi*, raw fish on specially prepared rice. Also *sashimi* or raw fish expertly sliced and served plain.
8. **Pufferfish Cuisine**: *Fugu*, full-course pufferfish meals.

Grilled Specialties

9. **Barbecued Chicked Pubs**: *Yakitori*, charcoal grilled chicken and other specialties on bamboo skewers. Also *kushi-yaki* or skewered and charcoal grilled delicacies.
10. **Hearthside Grills**: *Robatayaki*, fireside charcoal grilled fish, vegetables and other delicacies.
11. **Broiled Eel Cuisine**: *Unagi*, grilled Japanese eel. Also *dojo*, a small eel-like fish.

Casseroles and Stews

12. **Casserole Kitchens**: *Kamameshi*, rice casserole specialties with vegetables, fish and meat toppings.
13. **Cauldron Cuisines**: *Nabemono*, one-pot or bouillabaisse-like specialties. A favorite variation of *sumo* wrestlers in *chanko-nabe*.
14. **Dumpling-and-Broth Pubs**: *Oden*, steeped-in-broth fishcakes and vegetables.

Deep Fried Specialties

15. **Seafood and Vegetable Restaurants**: *Tempura*, light batter-coated deep-fried seafood and vegetable specialties.

16. **Pork Cutlet Shops**: *Tonkatsu*, deep-fried pork cutlets. Also *kushi-age* or deep-fried bread coated skewers of meats and vegetables.

Noodles and Do-it-Yourself Pizza
17. **Do-it-Yourself Pizzaria**: *Okonomiyaki*, thick griddlecakes you can cook yourself containing meat and seafood (literally, "as-you-like-it" specialties).
18. **Japanese Noodle Makers**: *Soba/Udon*, slender buckwheat and thick round wheat noodles. Also handmade *te-uchi* noodles.

The Ten Major Restaurant Centers in Tokyo

Just as New York's restaurants are hidden away in Chinatown, Little Italy, and the Greenwich Village cafe district, Tokyo's restaurants congregate in certain entertainment and business districts. There are, in fact ten major restaurant centers, each with its own distinctive character. Because they are located within a 12-minute walk from a major subway station, the districts are both convenient and bursting with activity. In alphabetical order (just as you will find them in the MAP section), the ten restaurant centers are:

1. Akasaka (see page 170)
Business center by day and glittering cabaret center by night, it boasts several towering hotels and the glamor of the famous personalities of the Tokyo Broadcasting System (the TBS television network). Akasaka is catered to by the largest concentration in Tokyo of typically Japanese *kappo* restaurants.

2. Asakusa (see page 176)
The most traditional and colorful part of old Tokyo is famous for the Kaminarimon Gate (with its king-size

Wind & Thunder Gods, 4.5 meter paper lantern and sandals), Nakamise souvenir shops lining the approach to Sensoji Temple (known as Asakusa Kannon Temple), and the 5-storey Dempoin Pagoda. Also, it is the home of the Japan Sumo Association (which arranges 15-day tournaments in Tokyo in January, May and September), and site of several major festivals such as the Sanja Festival (May 17–18), Night Festival (2nd Sunday in June) and Ground Cherry Fair with hundreds of outdoor stalls (July 9–10).

3. Ginza (see page 180)

By day, this 17th century center (*za*) of shogunate silver (*gin*) coin-making is now the most fashionable shopping center in Japan with many noted art and antique galleries and boutiques. By night, it is one of the largest entertainment districts, and full of expensive bars and cabarets, with by far the largest concentration of Japanese restaurants anywhere. Considered the gourmet center of Japan, Ginza is split east/west by Chuo Dori (a pedestrian mall on Sunday) and north/south by Harumi Dori (running from Yurakucho to the Harumi exhibition grounds).

Yurakucho, a popular movie, entertainment and shopping district located west of Ginza is with the famous Imperial Hotel and its panoramic rooftop view of Tokyo, which is best enjoyed at night.

4. Nihombashi (see page 200)

In the 17th century, the first Shogun, Tokugawa Ieyasu, built a wooden bridge (*hashi*) at the geographic center of Tokyo and hence, of Japan (*nihon*). Today, Nihombashi is a business, shopping and restaurant district.

Tokyo station, located west of Nihombashi near the Tokyo Stock Exchange (Kabutocho) and the Central Bank of Japan (Mitsukoshimae), is the terminus of west-bound Shinkansen "bullet" trains. On the east side, the Yaesu district offers many attractions, including an underground shopping arcade for travellers, with many restaurants and pubs. Beyond it, lies Nihombashi. On the west side is Marunouchi with its station facade modelled after the Amsterdam Central Station. The business districts of Marunouchi and Otemachi border the Imperial Palace.

5. Roppongi (see page 208)
Once a forest preserve (*Roppongi* means "six trees"), Roppongi is by day the home of record companies, creative boutiques, fashion studios and many foreign embassies. By night it is a youth mecca offering jazz, pubs, discotheques and nightclubs.

6. Shibuya (see page 212)
This major shopping and entertainment area is always full of crowds heading for the department stores (like Parco with its Restaurant City and the do-it-yourself emporium, Tokyu Hands), movie houses, game parlors and a planetarium. Shibuya station, which is the terminus for the Ginza subway line and Inokashira and Toyoko railway lines, is the meeting place for practically everyone (in front of the famous dog statue, in Hachiko Square).

7. Shimbashi (see page 222)
Adjoining Ginza to the south and within easy walking distance, Shimbashi is a business district which provides many of the nighttime features of the Ginza, but without the class or high prices. Restaurants and culinary hideaways abound.

8. Shinjuku (see page 226)
Designed as a subcenter of Tokyo with a huge railway station at its center, Shinjuku presents Tokyo's distinctive skyscraper skyline on the west side, with restaurants located in building basements and upper

floors. The top floor of the Keio Plaza Hotel offers an excellent panoramic view of Tokyo. Shinjuku also boasts many department stores (also with restaurants on the upper floors) and a sprawling underground shopping promenade which, we might add, can be navigated easily with the MAPS in this book.

9. Tsukiji (see page 240)
Site of the largest fish market in the world (and consequently, some of the best sushi restaurants), located east of Ginza and just past the Kabukiza Theater. Also home of the Hindu-style Honganji Temple of Kyoto's Jodo Buddhist Sect.

10. Ueno (see page 244)
This cultural haven contains several museums (the Western Art Museum designed by Le Corbusier, Japan's leading fine arts gallery as well as the National Science Museum), the Festival Hall for the performing arts, Tokyo University of Art, Ueno Zoo with its famous panda bear, and Tokyo's largest park. Ueno is the rail terminus to northern Japan and transfer point to the Keisei line going to Narita International Airport. Ueno's Ameyoko Dori is an extensive open-air market for bargain hunters.

Restaurants, Restaurants Everywhere, and Maps to Get You There

To the common lament of the tourist in Japan about being unable to read the characters on signs, this Guide replies with the most detailed, easy-to-use and complete set of maps ever offered the traveller. They are the first set of maps in English to list the signs you can read: the English signs on buildings. The maps also document Tokyo's extensive underground meccas. Buildings, alleyways, English language landmarks and subway exits are indicated, since in Tokyo, simple addresses invariably baffle the cornerside constabulary, not to mention the taxi driver.

With these maps, you need neither ask passersby for directions in broken Japanese nor have to cope with vague answers. This book gives you all the information you need to navigate Tokyo using the subways—the fastest, cheapest, quickest and safest in the world. Just get off at your stop, find the well-marked exit and head for the restaurant with guidebook in hand.

To help you find your way out of the station, it is useful to know six *kanji* characters found in station signs. They are surprisingly easy to remember with the mnemonics provided below. The box □ (*guchi*) stands for exit or entrance.

Central　中央口　*Chuo guchi*.
Square with a line through the center.

West　西口　*Nishi guchi*.
Square decanter bottle with a cork, like one you might find in the "wild West".

North　北口　*Kita guchi*.
A left-pointing fork in front of the letter "t".

South　南口　*Minami guchi*.
A gate open at the south, with a Yen-sign inside and a plus sign on top.

East　東口　*Higashi guchi*.
A telephone pole with a square pinned to the middle: originally, the rising sun in the east seen through the branches of a tree, which has two legs on the bottom for roots. This character is also found in the word *Tokyo* (東京), the "Eastern" capital.

Exit　出口　*Deguchi*.
Exit sign (yellow with black letters): a two-storey W-

shaped mountain.

Entrance 入口 *Iriguchi*.
Entrance (white with black letter): a square or open mouth, with an inverted V-shape (for a person walking) in front of it.

Spotting a Restaurant Amidst a Sea of Japanese Street Signs

Spotting a restaurant amidst a sea of shop signs all in Japanese can be trying for the uninitiated. But knowing the difference between a teahouse and a bathhouse can be crucial. There are clues, and a subtle code which is introduced here.

The most common restaurant symbol is a small curtain or *noren* which hangs in the upper part of a doorway. *Noren* are almost exclusive to the restaurant business and are hung in the doorway only when the restaurant is open. Where in other countries, restaurants use a "Yes, We're Open" sign, the Japanese use a *noren*. Navy blue and white *noren* characterize seafood, noodle and *kappo* restaurants, black and white are common for *tonkatsu*, and red for Chinese food establishments.

Rustic features also symbolize restaurants. For example, waterwheels, a tiny bamboo grove of live trees, a path of stones, a birdbath, or a wooden storefront. If you come across one of these features in an otherwise bustling neon environment, chances are that you have found a Japanese restaurant. Most restaurant fronts of this type also have a box-like lantern sign announcing the restaurant's name in black characters handwritten on a pane of white glass which is lit from behind.

Red paper lantern (*akachochin*, both round and cylindrical) are hung outside *yakitori* restaurants and pubs. They are usually marked with the four *hiragana* letters for *yakitori*, namely, やきとり or in Chinese characters 焼き鳥.

Some restaurants use an animal trademark to indicate what kind of food they serve, such as:

Blowfish: *Fugu* restaurants
Cow: *Sukiyaki*, *Teppanyaki*, *Shabu-shabu*
Crab: *Kani* restaurants
Pig: *Tonkatsu* restaurants
Pot-bellied Badger: Restaurants serving liquor

Some restaurants use the cooking pots or shape of the stoves as a symbol. For example:

The *robata* grill of *robatayaki* restaurants
The *kama* pot of *kamameshi* restaurants
The *nabe* stew-pot of *nabemono* restaurants

Certain written characters are easy to remember and are widely used in restaurant names such as:

The *u* う of *unagi* うなぎ
The *shi* し of *sushi* すし
The *ten* 天 of *tempura* 天ぷら
The *tori* 鳥 of *yakitori* 焼き鳥
The *so* そ of *soba* そば
The "center" 中 of a Chinese (Central Kingdom) restaurant 中華

Purple or orange signs, on the other hand, point to cheap bar or *snacku*. In busy entertainment districts, look for rustic landmarks, and you'll be safe from pawing hostesses, barroom crooning of the *karaoke* sing-it-yourself pubs and, of course, the Western hamburger.

Phrases for Ordering and Charts for Reading Japanese

Many visitors to Japan tell of being wined and dined on delicious Japanese foods as guests of a major trading firm, but of being unable to order the same meal when they returned on their own. The problem is simple: they can't read the Japanese menu. To solve this, most of the 18 major Japanese cuisines mentioned in this book are accompanied by a standard menu of entrees normally served by that type of restaurant. However, you can get a good meal anywhere, quickly and efficiently, if you are able to use a few Japanese phrases. Some of the crucial ones are listed below for you to use. (Notes: The *kudasai*, "please give me some", after an item or phrase turns it into a polite request. For a list of food words, turn to the GLOSSARY OF JAPANESE FOOD WORDS on page 251.)

Phrases for Ordering

Complete meal (table d'hote)	*Teishoku o kudasai* 定食をください
Usually in 3 standard grades: Regular	*Nami o kudasai* 並をください
Choice (more entrees)	*Jo o kudasai* 上をください
Special (most)	*Tokujo o kudasai* 特上をください
"Assortment" of popular items	*Moriawase o kudasai* 盛り合わせをください
"At the chef's pleasure"	*Omakase shimasu* おまかせします

"Special of the day"	*Higawari o kudasai* 日替りをください
Lunchbox (*obento*) with an assortment of items	*Obento o kudasai* お弁当をください
"The same as ~ " (and point to what the person next to you is eating)	*Onaji mono o kudasai* 同じ物をください
"What food is in season?"	*Shun no mono wa nan deska?* しゅんの物は何ですか
"Okay, I'll take it"	*Sore o kudasai* それをください
"Please give me ~ "	*~ o kudasai* ～をください
Coffee	*Kohi* コーヒー
Japanese tea	*Ocha* お茶
Black tea	*Kocha* 紅茶
Water	*Mizu* 水
Knife and fork	*Knifu to fooku* ナイフとフォーク
Spoon	*Supoon* スプーン
Chopsticks	*Hashi* はし
Menu	*Menu* メニュー
Hand towel	*Oshibori* おしぼり
"More please" (second helping)	*Okawari o kudasai* おかわりをください
A little	*Skoshi* すこし
"How long will it take?"	*Jikan wa dono gurai kakarimaska* 時間はどの位かかりますか
"Please rush the order"	*Iso-ide kudasai* 急いでください

Dining Phrases

Announcing that you will begin eating ("bon appetite")	*Itadakimas* いただきます
"Very delicious"	*Totemo oishi des* とてもおいしいです
"I appreciated the dinner"	*Gochisosama deshta* ごちそうさまでした
"Waiter!"	*Sumimasen* すみません
"Yes", "No"	*Hai* はい, *Iie* いいえ
"No more thanks"	*Kekko des* けっこうです
"How much for the meal?"	*O-ikura deska* おいくらですか
"Do you accept credit cards?"	*Kureditto Kaado wa tsukae maska* クレジット・カードは 使えますか
"Please give me a receipt"	*Ryoshusho o kudasai* 領収書をください

When ordering dishes or items from a menu, a different set of numbers for one to ten is used:

Hitotsu ————— one dish or item
Futatsu ————— two dishes or items
Mittsu ————— three dishes or items
Yottsu ————— four dishes or items
Itsutsu ————— five dishes or items
Muttsu ————— six dishes or items
Nanatsu ————— seven dishes or items
Yattsu ————— eight dishes or items
Kokonotsu —— nine dishes or items
Toh ————— ten dishes or items

For the person who wants to make the extra effort and give the Japanese "alphabets" a crack, use the KANA ALPHABET FINDER for *hiragana* and *katakana* characters (next page) to try reading the Japanese menu itself or signs on the plastic food displays. (Note: The next page can be removed for carrying in your billfold.) The Japanese numbers are also easy to read. Try it after looking through the memory aids provided below.

The even numbers 2-4-6-8-10 each have a pair of strokes and are symmetrical:

二	2 *Ni*
四	4 *Shi* or *Yon*
Angles in the upper corners of a box	
六	6 *Roku*
Looks like a man's head and arms with a pair of legs	
八	8 *Hachi*
Looks like the pair of legs by itself	
十	10 *Ju*
A plus sign	

The first two odd numbers are a give-away, and the rest coincidentally contain the pattern of the letter "T."

一	1 *Ichi*
三	3 *San*
五	5 *Go*
Looks liked the letter "h" between two parallel lines	
七	7 *Nana* or *Shichi*
Looks like the letter "t"	
九	9 *Ku* or *kyu*
A plus sign with the capital letter "L" attached in front of it	

●Kana Alphabet Finder

Hiragana Chart

	1 Stroke	2 Strokes	3 and 4 Strokes
Loops	の no る ru	め me み mi ね ne ぬ nu よ yo す su　ず zu	あ a お o ま ma む mu な na は ha　ば ba　ぱ pa ほ ho　ぼ bo　ぽ po
Spaces		え e い i う u ら ra り ri こ ko　ご go	に ni か ka　が ga け ke　げ ge き ki　ぎ gi さ sa　ざ za た ta　だ da ふ fu　ぶ bu　ぷ pu
Others	ん -n ろ ro く ku　ぐ gu し shi　じ ji そ so　ぞ zo て te　で de つ tsu　づ zu へ he　べ be　ぺ pe ひ hi　び bi　ぴ pi	れ re わ wa ゆ yu ち chi　ぢ ji と to　ど do	も mo を o (wo) や ya せ se　ぜ ze

Rules: ろ ＝ 1 stroke,　ゆ ＝ 2 strokes,　が ＝ 3 strokes

Katakana Chart

	1 Stroke	2 Strokes	3 and 4 Strokes
Crosses		メ me ナ na ヌ nu ヤ ya カ ka　ガ ga セ se　ゼ ze	オ o モ mo チ chi　ヂ ji キ ki　ギ gi サ sa　ザ za ホ ho　ボ bo　ポ po
Spaces		ン -n ニ ni ラ ra リ ri ル ru ハ ha　バ ba　パ pa ソ so　ゾ zo	ミ mi シ shi　ジ ji テ te　デ de ツ tsu　ヅ zu
Others	ノ no レ re フ fu　ブ bu　プ pu ヘ he　ベ be　ペ pe ー long vowel sign.	ア a イ i マ ma ム mu ヲ o (wo) ワ wa ユ yu コ ko　ゴ go ク ku　グ gu ス su　ズ zu ト to　ド do ヒ hi　ビ bi　ピ pi	エ e ウ u ネ ne ロ ro ヨ yo ケ ke　ゲ ge タ ta　ダ da

Rules: フ = 1 stroke,　ロ = 3 strokes,　ガ = 2 strokes

百　100 *Hyaku*
A box with a pin inside and a short "T" on top

千　1,000 *Sen*
A plus sign, as in the *kanji* number 10, with a sloping roof above it

万　10,000 *Man*
Looks like the letter "h" with a roof on top

Cuisines Symbols

General Restaurants

Regional Specialty Houses,
Kyodo-ryori

General Style,
Nihon-ryori

Seasonal Restaurants

Japanese Haute Cuisine,
Kaiseki

Cordon-Bleu Restaurants,
Kappo

Beef

Beef-Saute/Fondue
Restaurants,
Sukiyaki/Shabu-shabu

Steak Grills,
Teppanyaki

Seafood

Fresh Seafood Cuisines,
Sushi

Crab Specialties,
Kani

Pufferfish Cuisine,
Fugu

Grilled specialties

Barbecued Chicken Pubs,
Yakitori/Kushiyaki

Hearthside Grills,
Robatayaki

Broiled Eel Cuisine,
Unagi

Casseroles and Stews

Casserole Kitchens,
Kamameshi

Cauldron Cuisines,
Nabemono/Chanko-nabe

Dumpling-and-Broth Pubs,
Oden

Deep-Fried Specialties

Seafood and Vegetable
Restaurants,
Tempura

Pork Cutlet Shops,
Tonkatsu/Kushi-age

Noodles and Do-It-Yourself Pizza

Do-It-Yourself Pizzeria,
Okonomiyaki

Japanese Noodle Makers,
Soba/Udon

Handmade Noodles,
Te-uchi

● Regional Specialty Houses:
Kyodo-Ryori

For those who can afford the time to travel throughout Japan's mountainous archipelago, cities and towns all over Japan offer an incredibly rich and appetizing variety of gastronomical delicacies for the gourmet, far beyond the range of "typically Japanese foods" such as *sukiyaki*, *oden* and *tempura* which are actually the specialities of the Tokyo region. For the average person who's time is more limited, *kyodo-ryori* or regional cuisines which can be found in Tokyo restaurants provide an accessible alternative and a delicious adventure.

●
The Regional Cooking of Japan

Regional dishes are classed as a kind of *inaka-ryori* (or country-style cooking). They developed mainly in pre-industrial times when cities and towns were isolated by infrequent transportation and communication links, and use of local produce raised, grown or caught nearby was the norm. In those times, preparation of local dishes was considered a matter of local pride and personal achievement. Even the names of local dishes, which mainly describe ingredients and are totally devoid of sales appeal, reflect this homely origin.

In modern times, inter-regional transport and even foreign trade have reduced the necessity of using local produce. However, the specialty dishes of the region remain on the menu, supported by the availability of local products and home teaching of traditional culinary skills.

Cuisines which are available in Tokyo are listed below for each of the eight administrative regions of Japan. These cuisines, however, are often known by their pre-industrial regional names which are still in use even though the official names of the regions themselves have changed.

●

Regions of Japan and Cuisine Names

Honshu (the largest and main island of Japan) is divided into 5 regions which run from north to south as follows:

Region	Location	Cuisines Names
2–Tohoku	Northern area	*Akita*, *Michinoku* (Aomori)
3–Kanto	The area surrounding Tokyo	—
4–Chubu	Central area	*Hokuriku*, *Hida* (Gifu), *Echigo* (Niigata)
5–Kinki	The area surrounding Osaka	*Kyo*, *Kamigata*
6–Chugoku	Southern area	*Hiroshima*, *Shimane*

● Regions of Japan

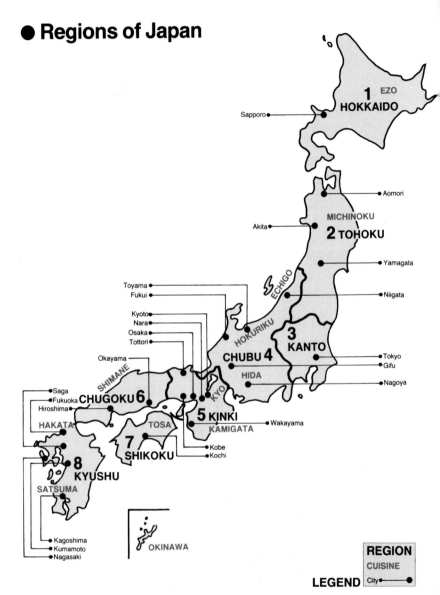

- **1 HOKKAIDO** — EZO
  - Sapporo
- **2 TOHOKU** — MICHINOKU
  - Aomori
  - Akita
  - Yamagata
  - Niigata
- **3 KANTO**
  - Tokyo
  - Gifu
  - Nagoya
- **4 CHUBU** — HIDA, ECHIGO, HOKURIKU
  - Toyama
  - Fukui
- **5 KINKI** — KAMIGATA, KYO
  - Kyoto
  - Nara
  - Osaka
  - Tottori
  - Wakayama
  - Kobe
  - Kochi
- **6 CHUGOKU** — SHIMANE
  - Okayama
  - Hiroshima
- **7 SHIKOKU** — TOSA
- **8 KYUSHU** — HAKATA, SATSUMA
  - Saga
  - Fukuoka
  - Kagoshima
  - Kumamoto
  - Nagasaki

OKINAWA

LEGEND

| REGION |
| CUISINE |
| City●————● |

The remaining 3 regions are the other major islands of Japan:

1–Hokkaido	Northern island	*Ezo*
7–Shikoku	Southern island boundary of the Inland Sea	*Tosa* (Kochi)
8–Kyushu	Southern island (Okinawa is classed here also)	*Hakata* (Fukuoka), *Kumamoto*, Satsuma (Kagoshima), *Saga*, *Okinawa*

Recognizing a Regional Restaurant

Although some regional restaurants display regional symbols, for example, a bear with a salmon in its mouth for Hokkaido, regional symbols are so "Japanese" that *kyodo-ryori* restaurants can scarcely be distinguished by them from any other Japanese restaurant. So just continue looking for rustic items like a waterwheel, stone path, water fountain, etc. to find a *kyodo-ryori* restaurant.

◄ Country-style restaurant front

Atmosphere and Service

A *kyodo-ryori* restaurant's decor is designed to look and feel as it it were small country restaurant buried in the heart of the region itself. Costumes are authentic and regional handicrafts adorn the walls. Some find the atmosphere so inviting that go on to visit the region, while others make it a habit to re-visit the restaurant over and over again in order to find refuge from the city.

▲ Handicraft atmosphere of a regional restaurant (*Kyodo-ryori*)

Ordering from the Kyodo-Ryori Menu

Ordering regional cuisines is a snap if you don't get sidetracked by the infinite variety of offerings. We suggest that you pick a food category, consult the list of restaurants for one nearby, and order only the most famous dish. Stews bring out the best of many ingredients, and it is the unusual ingredient, the local fish or mountain green, for instance, which is the hallmark of a region's cookery. *Sukiyaki* is a variety of stew which has many well-known regional variations such as *udon-suki* (with *udon* noodles), *kani-suki* (with crab) and *uo-suki* (with fish).

Most stews fall into the *nabemono* category. The *nabe* is the ideal combination of stewing pot and serving dish (see color photo on page 153). The stock or broth of the *nabemono* varies greatly from region to region. Some are fish-based, some seaweed-based, and near Nara the locals even use milk-and-butter broth for chicken stew. However, the most common stock or soup (*shiru*) base is made of (*miso*) soybean in which case the stews are called *misonabe*. Whatever the broth is used, be sure to ladle some into your dish to enjoy as a rich soup.

●
Famous Stews of Japan

Here are some of the more renowned regional stews worth sampling:

Main Ingredient	Kyodo dish	Region No.	Region Name
Beef	Miso suki みそすき		Throughout Japan
Clam	Fukagawa-nabe 深川なべ	3	Tokyo
Crab	Kani-suki かにすき	4	Fukui

Crab	Kawari kani nabe かわりかになべ	1	Hokkaido
Chicken	Asuka-nabe 飛鳥なべ	5	Nara
Chicken	Mizutaki 水炊き	8	Fukuoka
Duck	Kamo-nabe かもなべ	5	Shiga
Fish	Dongara jiru どんがら汁	2	Yamagata
Fish	Uo-suki 魚すき	5	Osaka
Fish	Tsumire jiru つみれ汁	1	Hokkaido
Fish and mochi	Shuhei-nabe しゅうへいなべ	8	Nagasaki
Horse meat	Sakura-nabe さくらなべ	3	Tokyo
Loach and eggs	Yanagawa-nabe 柳川なべ	8	Fukuoka
Loach and leeks	Dojo-nabe どじょうなべ		Throughout Japan
Oysters	Dote-nabe 土手なべ	6	Hiroshima
Oysters	Kaki no miso nabe カキのみそなべ	6	Hiroshima
Pig/Boar	Inobuta-nabe いのぶたなべ	4	Shizuoka

Rice	Kiritampo きりたんぽ	2	Akita
Salmon	Ishikari-nabe 石狩なべ	1	Hokkaido
Salmon	Aki-aji-nabe あきあじなべ	1	Hokkaido
Salmon	Sake no kasu nabe 鮭のかすなべ	1	Hokkaido
Salmon	Sampei jiru 三平汁	1	Hokkaido
Seafood	Kaizoku-ryori 海賊料理	5	Mie
Sweet potato	Imoko-nabe いもこなべ	2	Yamagata
Udon noodles	Okirikomi おきりこみ	3	Gunma
Udon noodles	Hoto-nabe ほうとうなべ	4	Yamanashi
Udon noodles	Udon-suki うどんすき	5	Osaka
Vegetables	Noppei jiru のっぺい汁	4	Niigata
Wild boar	Tanzawa botan-nabe 丹沢ぼたんなべ	3	Kanagawa
Wild boar	Shishi-nabe ししなべ	4	Shizuoka
Wild Boar	Botan-nabe ぼたんなべ	5	Hyogo

Famous Fish and Rice Dishes of Japan

In addition to stews, the most famous regional foods are variations of fish and rice. In addition to stews, the most famous regional foods are variations of fish and rice. Rice dishes fall, for the most part into the *kamameshi* category (see the **KAMAMESHI** chapter on page 104), while fish dishes are classified as sushi. The most popular *sushi* dish, after *nigiri-zushi* is the *sushi* variation called *oshi-zushi* (pressed *sushi*), *hako-zushi* (box *sushi*) or *Osaka-zushi*. The names refer to the method which originated in Osaka, of preparing the rice balls by pressing rice into wooden forms.

A regional variation on sushi which looks very attractive is *sugata-zushi*, or "natural shape" *sushi*. In this style, fish is placed on rice so that it maintains its original shape and outline as a fish.

▲ Natural-shape *sushi* (*Sugata-zushi*)

Common *sugata-zushi* are the following:

Ayu no sugata-zushi from Tottori (Region 5) using sweet smelt.

Kamasu no sugata-zushi from Fukuoka (Region 8) using pike.

Saba no sugata-zushi from Wakayama (Region 5) using mackerel.

Samma no sugata-zushi from Mie (Region 5) using Pacific saury

Some of the well-known regional fish and rice dishes are listed below:

Dish	Description	Region No.	Region Name
Battera ばってら	Marinated mackerel pressed on top of rice	5	Osaka
Chinu-meshi ちぬめし	A whole steamed fish atop rice	7	Kagawa
Funa-zushi ふなずし	Pickled fish served without rice	5	Kyoto
Ishikari-zushi 石狩ずし	Bamboo-leaf packets of seafood sashimi	1	Hokkaido
Kenuki-zushi 毛抜きずし	Sushi wrapped in bamboo leaves	4	Nagoya
Masu-zushi ますずし	Bamboo leaf with rice and fish on top of it	4	Toyama
Matsuri-zushi 祭りずし	A "festival" of seafood colors and textures	6	Okayama

Omura-zushi 大村ずし	Fish sandwiched between rice and an omelette	8	Nagasaki
Tsuya-zushi つやずし	Double-decker layers of fish on rice	5	Mie
Yuzu-meshi ゆずめし	A cooked seafood feast atop rice	5	Tottori

Sashimi too has its regional variations:

Kibinago no sashimi from Kyushu (Region 8): A gorgeous tinsel-like display by a platter full of blue sprat.

Budo ebi no sashimi from Miyagi (Region 2): A sculptured garden of prawns.

Katsuo no tataki from Kochi (Region 7): A mouthwatering platter of lightly brazed bonito.

▲ Handicraft atmosphere of a regional restaurant (*Kyodo-ryori*)

Grilled Combination Seafood Platter Favorites

This list of regional specialties goes on and on and fills volumes. As a closing recommendation, we list our favorite, grilled, combination seafood platters:

Seafood Platter	Region No.	Region Name
Genpei yaki 源平焼き	7	Kagawa
Gocha yaki ごちゃ焼き	1	Hokkaido
Ishihama yaki いしはま焼き	8	Fukuoka

Recommended Restaurants

Type of Food	Zone	Restaurant Name	Map-Rest. No.	Floor
Akita	Ginza	☆ AKITA-YA	9–9	5F
Hakata-Mizutaki	Roppongi	☆ SHIN MIURA	20–11	B1
Hida	Roppongi	☆ SHIRAKAWA	20–3	1F
Hokkaido	Ginza	☆ SAPPORO	8–9	B1
Hokkaido	Shibuya	☆ OHOTSUKU	24–12	3F
Hokkaido	Shinjuku	☆ YUKKU	29–11	50F
Hoppo	Shibuya	☆ MATSUMAE	22–4	B1
Kagoshima	Shinjuku	☆ KURAWANKA	34–16	B1
Satsuma	Shinjuku	☆ SHAMO	32–8	8F
Tosa	Akasaka	☆ NEBOKE	2–8	1F
Tosa	Ginza	☆ NEBOKE	14–6	1F
Tosa	Shibuya	☆ NEBOKE	26–15	2F
Tosa	Shinjuku	☆ NEBOKE	29–5	50F
Tosa	Tsukiji	☆ YOSHIMOTO	37–9	1F

● General Restaurants:
Nihon-Ryori

Family restaurants in Japan? Well, almost. Restaurants that serve *nihon-ryori* (which literally means "Japanese foods") offer *sushi*, *tempura*, the ubiquitous gourmet lunch box known as *obento*, *sukiyaki*, and more. Where other restaurants specialize in one style of cooking, these restaurants serve a variety of specialties suitable for the whole family. Although somewhat similar to *kappo* restaurants in the range of dishes, *nihon-ryori-ya* are less gourmet and cater more to the daytime crowd and women. Their atmosphere is ideal for having a lunchtime chat with a friend during a shopping spree. Consequently, the restaurants are usually found in shopping districts and in the upper floor of department stores.

Some *nihon-ryori-ya* emphasize their serene Japanese atmosphere, in which case they are refered to as *wafu* or "Japanese style".

Other *nihon-ryori* restaurants stress the thoroughly Japanese nature of the cuisine by referring to their dishes as *washoku*. Still others, which serve mostly seasonal foods, are called *kisetsu*. All have menus designed to please your taste.

For guidance on ordering, turn to the **RESTAURANT FINDER** to find the section on your favorite Japanese food in this book.

◀ Typical general
restaurant dishes

Recommended Restaurants

Type of Food	Zone	Restaurant Name	Map-Rest. No.	Floor
Kansai-kappo	Ginza	☆ CHINZANSO	12–24	B1
Kansai-kappo	Ginza	☆ GENNAI	12–27	B1
Kansai-kappo	Ginza	☆ HAMASAKU HONTEN	12–29	1F
Kansai-kappo	Ginza	☆ OGURA	13–12	B1
Kansai-kappo	Ginza	☆ HAMAMURA	15–4	1F
Kansai-kappo	Nihombashi	☆ SANGEN	17–10	4F
Kisetsu	Ginza	☆ IZUMI	8–8	B1
Kisetsu	Nihombashi	☆ OTAKUBO	19–1	B1
Kisetsu	Shibuya	☆ HAYASHI	23–8	2F
Kisetsu	Shinjuku	☆ IMASA	33–1	1F
Kisetsu	Shinjuku	☆ MATSUZUMI	34–12	8F
Kisetsu	Ueno	☆ TAKEBUN	38–9	1F
Nihon-ryori	Ginza	☆ IMAHAN	8–2	B1
Nihon-ryori	Ginza	☆ SHIRU NAO	8–17	9F
Nihon-ryori	Ginza	☆ ASUKA	9–10	4F
Nihon-ryori	Ginza	☆ KINSEN	9–12	5F
Nihon-ryori	Ginza	☆ TSUKIJI TAMURA	10–9	8F
Nihon-ryori	Ginza	☆ TSUBOHAN	12–5	1F
Nihon-ryori	Ginza	☆ OSHIMA	13–2	8F
Nihon-ryori	Ginza	☆ KACHO	13–5	B2
Nihon-ryori	Ginza	☆ TSUKIJI UEMURA	13–15	7F
Nihon-ryori	Ginza	☆ MUNAKATA	14–19	B1
Nihon-ryori	Nihombashi	☆ KAMOGAWA	16–8	B1
Nihon-ryori	Nihombashi	☆ MUNAKATA	16–15	B1
Nihon-ryori	Nihombashi	☆ UZURA	17–15	B1
Nihon-ryori	Shinjuku	☆ ASHIBI	29–15	2F
Nihon-ryori	Shinjuku	☆ TSUKIJI UEMURA	30–18	53F
Nihon-ryori	Shinjuku	☆ YOIGOKORO	32–10	B1
Nihon-ryori	Shinjuku	☆ FUNE	32–11	5F
Wafu	Shinjuku	☆ KOSHIKIJIMA	29–3	51F
Washoku	Shinjuku	☆ SETO-UCHI	29–9	50F

● Japanese Haute Cuisine:
Kaiseki

Kaiseki is as much an art form as a style of cooking and food preparation. A *kaiseki* meal is imbued with the spiritual hush of the tea ceremony, its serene balance of food and utensil, and the visual celebration of nature's delicious bounty. Through five centuries, *kaiseki*'s master chefs have preserved and passed on the secrets of their tranquil art, and knowledge of the harvest and spawning cycles of all manners of flora and fauna. They have set the standards of "Japanese" gourmet cooking. A *kaiseki* meal is the tongue-tingling zenith of the Japanese dining experience (see color photo on page 154).

●
The History of Kaiseki

In 1749, the eighth Shogun, Yoshimasa Ashikaga, built a small, rustic teahouse which is now part of the Ginkakuji Temple in Kyoto. In its secluded environment he entertained guests, using exquisite utensils from foreign lands in the preparation of green tea (*cha*).

At first, the tea ceremony (*cha-no-yu*) which developed was the leisure pastime of nobility and the wealthy because of the large investment in a teahouse and elegant utensils. However, as time passed, a more humble version of the tea ceremony called *wabizuki* was developed, because hospitality and attention to detail were felt to be more important than the opulent displays popularized by Yoshimasa. Thus it became possible for anyone to participate in the tea ceremony.

With the tea ceremony, there developed a small meal of a few choice morsels. These minimalist dishes were called *kaiseki* since the meal was similar in purpose to the warm stones (*seki*) which Buddhist priests put in their robes: to forget their empty stomachs (*kai*) while studying and meditating. *Kaiseki* restaurants and their Kyoto variants, the *kyo-ryori* restaurants, remain today

▲ Tea ceremony room of a *kaiseki* restaurant

one of the main learning centers for the art of the tea ceremony.

Although the name *kaiseki* reveals its Buddhist roots, the essence of the food service comes from traditional Japanese *Shinto* beliefs regarding the primacy of nature. The four seasons and seasonal foods are the cornerstones.

It is said that a Japanese meal is a communion with nature. You will note that ingredients are all natural, of high quality, absolutely fresh, and served in a simple, uncluttered manner which reflect their state in nature, undistorted by sauces. They are served with as little delay as possible after being prepared.

The Japanese believe that nature is the greatest artist. Design and display of food reflects nature's shapes—the islands, mountains, forests, leaves and flowers. The Japanese have made an art out of cutting and peeling foods into nature's shapes, an art called *mukimono*. Garnishes are used to symbolize the seasons and seasonal rituals, not just to bring out the flavors of dishes. As in nature, food displays contain contrasting elements of color, shape, flavor, consistency and texture and are arranged and presented on plates and bowls of varying shapes and textures. Repetition and its counterpart in art, symmetry, is consciously avoided, perhaps because it does not reflect the reality of nature which is change.

The *kaiseki* menu follows a seasonal cycle in keeping with the dictum of perfect freshness. This cycle starts in November when the year's first tea is ready for grinding. The year is then divided into the 12 months, each with a seasonal spirit reflecting Japanese customs and tradition. The kaiseki menu and tableware are varied according to this seasonal spirit. Thus when you order a course meal, you are sure to get the best seasonal food available in Japan.

The Kaiseki Seasonal Cycle

Month	Seasonal Spirit
November	Beginning anew
December	Cold, freshness
January	Hope for long life (symbolized by pines) and prosperity (symbolized by plums)
February	Anticipation
March	Women's spirit: orderliness
April	Spring, climax (symbolized by cherry blossoms)
May	Man's spirit: bravery and heartiness (symbolized by the spawning carp)
June	Escape, rest
July	Heat, zestiness
August	Penitence, fasting
September	Awe, mystery, reverence
October	Reflection, nostalgia, philosophical balance, transience

●

Recognizing a Kaiseki Restaurant

If in Japan you should find yourself in a peaceful, unimposing room whose stillness is punctuated only by the melodies of a *koto* player, then perhaps it is because you have wandered into a *kaiseki* restaurant. Rustic and tranquil, even in the center of such a great megalopolis as Tokyo, *kaiseki* restaurants remain hidden within skyscrapers and basements. The greatest clue to finding one is the quiet traffic of many *kimono* clad customers who flock to these repositories of culinary art, fine ceramicware and Japanese culture.

▲ Landscaped restaurant front

Atmosphere and Service

No matter what the season, *kaiseki* meals offer a succession of finely prepared delicacies designed to bring the diner tranquility and appease his appetite without awakening the passion of gluttony. As a Japanese proverb says, "a stomach four-fifth's full knows no doctors"—such is the wisdom of abstinence.

Each of the courses of a Kyoto-style *kaiseki* has a special name and standard style of cooking as listed below. All courses are served on beautiful handcrafted pottery and ceramic works of art. Kaiseki is one of the rare opportunities for a person to touch, weigh and dine upon antique dishes which might otherwise remain locked in a glass case in a museum. Hot *sake* is served when a course does not contain either a hot soup or tea.

◀ Haute-cuisine *kaiseki* service

Main Kaiseki Service

Gohan (located on the diner's left) ごはん
Freshly prepared rice to be tasted first, since rice is a symbol of life and beginnings.

Miso-shiru (located on the diner's right) みそ汁
Clear *miso* soup made with sweet white *miso* or *shiro miso* which is specially used in *kaiseki* as opposed to the red *miso* soup *(akadashi)* which is normally served in restaurants.

Muko-zuke 向付け
A tasty dish (usually of raw seafood, often *sashimi*); literally "located" *(zuke)* just "beyond" *(muko)* the first two dishes mentioned above.

Wan-mori 椀盛り
A clear broth in which the ingredients are "piled up" (from the verb *moru*) mountain-like and served in a lacquered bowl *(wan)*. Herbs related to the season —which is, after all, what "seasoning" is all about—are served along with the clear soup (also called *suimono*). Garnishes *(suikuchi)* float on top, through which *(kuchi)* one sips *(sui)* the soup, savoring its first taste impressions.

Yakimono 焼き物
A charcoal "broiled" entree

Hashi-arai 箸洗い
A flavorful "chopstick wash" consisting of a salty or sour plum soup (salt and plum being the Japanese characters for "seasoning") and other ingredients to reflect the mood of the season and the tea ceremony theme of gathering together.

Hassun 八寸
A special delicacy arranged artfully and assymetricaly on a small square tray (eight *ha* inches *sun* on a side)

Closing Service

Konomono 香の物
Pickled vegetables (literally "a fragrant thing") to refresh one's mouth.

Okashi お菓子
Sweets or fruit *(kudamono)* served in layered wooden boxes to prepare the mouth for the contrasting purity and bitterness of ground tea *(ryokucha)* which is to follow.

Ocha お茶
Green tea (tea in its natural state before it undergoes a fermentation process to turn it brown) served in a bowl after being whipped up ceremoniously from powder and hot water into a frothy brew.

Optional Kaiseki Service

Azuke-bachi 預け鉢
Two central dishes from which diners help themselves (literally, "entrusted bowls"). One is a hot simmered, steamed, deep-fried, or stewed dish and the other, by way of contrast, is a cold vinegared *(sunomono)* or dressed salad *(aizakana)*.

Shiizakana 強肴

An optional dish when "requested" or added to the meal, originally for when the host wished to display some particularly fine ceramic wares he had collected.

●
Ordering from the Kaiseki Menu

If you appreciate culinary delicacies, you'll love *kaiseki*. *Kaiseki* menus offer a cornucopia of gastronomical treats including tempura, cooked seasonal fish and even sirloin steak in some cases. (For menus, refer to through the **RESTAURANT FINDER** to chapters on **TEMPURA, SUSHI, UNAGI, TEPPANYAKI,** etc.) Since the cost runs as high as the quality, choose a set course according to your budget. Rest assured, that whatever you have, it will include the season's best offerings.

Recommended Restaurants

Type of Food	Zone	Restaurant Name	Map-Rest. No.	Floor
Kaiseki	Asakusa	☆ ICHIMATSU	4–30	1F
Kaiseki	Ginza	☆ KYOTARU	7–2	B1
Kaiseki	Ginza	☆ MATSUHANA	12–20	B1
Kaiseki	Ginza	☆ TSUJITOME	12–25	B1
Kaiseki	Shibuya	☆ HYO-TEI	22–10	8F
Kaiseki	Shibuya	☆ UEMURA	22–28	7F
Kaiseki	Shinjuku	☆ MIYAMA	29–18	45F
Kaiseki	Shinjuku	☆ KYOIZUMO-YA	30–13	B1
Kaiseki	Tsukiji	☆ TAKANO	37–10	1F
Kaiseki	Tsukiji	☆ UEMURA	36–3	1F
Kaiseki/fugu	Shinjuku	TAGAWA	32–17	1F
Kyo-kaiseki	Shinjuku	☆ KAKIDEN	34–14	6F
Kyo-ryori	Ginza	☆ AWATA	6–10	B1
Kyo-ryori	Ginza	TANGUMA	13–20	7F
Kyo-ryori	Shinjuku	☆ MINOKICHI	29–4	48F
Kyo-ryori	Shinjuku	☆ SHIMOGAMOSARYO	30–6	B2
Kyo-ryori	Shinjuku	KYUNOCHA-YA	31–10	10F

● Cordon-Bleu Restaurants:
Kappo

If you have had the privilege to dine at a fancy *geisha* house or glittering cabaret, chances are that the food was catered by the chef of a nearby *kappo* restaurant. The reason is simple. *Kappo* chefs are among the few who are able to provide the finest quality cuisines to match the best in Japanese VIP entertainment. Surprising as it may seem, you can enjoy the same quality food at moderate prices (albeit without the VIP entertainment) just by going to and dining in a *kappo* restaurant directly.

Kappo restaurants provide a Cordon-Bleu quality of food. Everything is *à la carte* and almost always available.

Like their formal *kaiseki* counterparts (see the chapter on **KAISEKI**, page 42), *kappo* chefs have the skill and training to prepare any and all of the best types of Japanese foods. Even the name *kappo* is quite general. Literally it is a compound of the words "cutting" (*katsu*) and "cooking" (*po*).

Although *kappo* restaurants are rarely large and appear to offer mainly a pub-like atmosphere, rest assured, your gourmet taste buds are in for a treat.

For guidance on ordering, just turn to the **RESTAURANT FINDER** to find your favorite chapter in this book.

▲ Badger statues in front of a *kappo* pub

Recommended Restaurants

Type of Food	Zone	Restaurant Name	Map-Rest. No.	Floor
Kappo	Akasaka	☆ OKUBO	2–13	1F
Kappo	Asakusa	☆ TATSUMIYA	5–7	1F
Kappo	Ginza	☆ SENJYU	7–12	1F
Kappo	Ginza	☆ OHKUMA	14–22	1F
Kappo	Ginza	☆ UMEMOTO	15–6	1F
Kappo	Ginza	☆ JIRO	15–7	1F
Kappo	Ginza	☆ SEKI-TEI	15–21	B1
Kappo	Shibuya	☆ SARUYAMA	23–11	2F
Kappo	Shibuya	☆ UEMURA	23–16	8F
Kappo	Shibuya	☆ GOEN-TEI	24–1	1F
Kappo	Shibuya	☆ TAMAKYU	24–8	1F
Kappo	Shibuya	☆ MASA	26–8	B1
Kappo	Shimbashi	☆ SU-EGEN	27–20	1F
Kappo	Shinjuku	☆ GINSA-AN	30–2	49F
Kappo	Tsukiji	☆ NAKATA	37–8	1F
Kappo	Ueno	☆ UEMURA	39–10	5F

● Beef Saute/Fondue Restaurants:
Sukiyaki and Shabu-Shabu

For the *fondue* afficionado who enjoys cooking food at the tableside as an intimate setting for conversation, the Japanese *sukiyaki* and *shabu-shabu* specialties are very popular. The meal begins with a display of the most delectable, thinly-sliced prime beef and exquisitely cut vegetables. These are set simmering in a shallow pan full of broth, right on your table (see color photo on page 157). When the steam grows thick and fragrant, each diner plunges his chopsticks into the dish searching for the perfect tidbit.

●

History of Sukiyaki

The folk etymology of *sukiyaki* is "plowshare" *(suki)* "grilling" *(yaki)*. When Buddhism became Japan's national religion in the 7th century, the eating of many animals was forbidden by decree of the Emperor. So in an effort to avoid defiling their everyday cooking wares, it is said that farmers were accustomed to roasting up meat on a plowshare. Another theory has it that the thick-bottomed flatiron skillet used in cooking *sukiyaki* was copied from the specialized pans used for falconry cooking *(takajo-ryori)*, but that due to sheer resemblance, the shallow cast-iron pan got its name from the plowshare.

At any rate, *sukiyaki*, like *shabu-shabu* and *teppan-yaki*, is a recent response to the Western diet. With the opening of the country to the foreign world, beef-eating was promoted by the government with almost religious zeal, as the mark of "an advanced civilization." Emperor Meiji even went so far as to issue a special statement in 1873 that the beef-eating taboo was an "irrational tradition."

Although today, Japanese eat steaks and hamburgers with gusto, a monument in Kakisaki (two miles east of Shimoda) which "marks the spot on which the first cow in Japan was slaughtered for human consumption," documents the "first" beef meal as a cultural sacrifice, made for the table of Townsend Harris, the first American Consul to Japan.

●
Recognizing a Sukiyaki Restaurant

Because beef is expensive in Japan, the restaurants that offer *sukiyaki*, *shabu-shabu* and *teppanyaki* are high-class establishments, advertised austerely with a standing square sign in Japanese outside the entrance. Suehiro has its signs in English, but for the most part, the only telltale identification for other establishments are the words in Japanese—*sukiyaki*, *shabu-shabu* or *teppanyaki*—or if you are lucky, a picture of a cow.

●
Atmosphere and Service

At more traditional restaurants, customers are served at specially designed low tables which sometimes have a space below floor level to accommodate long legs, although Western tables for four to six are also common. The atmosphere is quiet and refined, full only of the pungent smells and sounds of bubbling broth.

● Gourmet Tips

The beef used in *sukiyaki* and other Japanese dishes is the highest quality sirloin. It has a higher fat content than Westerners are accustomed to, perhaps because such cuts of meat rate four notches higher than USDA's rank, "choice". World famous of course, is Matsuzaka's "Kobe beef," produced from cattle who are massaged daily and fed beer, even protected from mosquitoes by the burning of joss sticks in order to have the tenderest marbled flesh possible (known as *shimofuri-niku*).

The food-lover might vary his fare by asking for his meat to be sauteed in butter, or marinated prior to cooking in a white wine mixture. Some regional variations of *sukiyaki* are also well worth trying.

Omi-niku no sukiyaki 近江肉のすき焼き
Omi beef from Otsu has a long history of being "Kobe quality" marbled beef, due to the fine water and wide-open ranches where the herds are bred.

Jingisukan-yaki ジンギスカン焼き
A variation of Genghis Khan (meat slices cooked in a Mongolian hotpot, see *shabu-shabu* below) comes from Sapporo. It is made with thinly sliced lamb, bell peppers and mushrooms.

● The Standard Fare

The standard order consists of courses, for each meal is served as a platter of ingredients. *Sukiyaki* platters include paper-thin slices of choice marbled beef *(gyu-niku)*, diagonally cut scallions *(negi)*, mushrooms, spinach *(horenso)*, trefoil *(mitsuba*, or marsh parsley), bean-curd *(tofu)*, bamboo shoots *(takenoko)*, chrysan-themum leaves *(shungiku)*, carrots *(ninjin)* and wheat gluten *(fu)*. If you want to order more of anything, just refer to the word above and say, *okawari o kudasai* ("Please may I have another serving of . . .").

Also served is a container of specially prepared sauce for simmering the meat which is a mixture of soy sauce, sweet sake, and *kombu* seaweed or grated skipjack. Each customer is given a bowl containing a raw egg, which is an excellent sweet dressing to the hot food and definitely worth trying.

●
Ordering from the Sukiyaki Menu

Sukiyaki and *shabu-shabu* restaurants offer the follow-ing selection of cuts of beef.

(Note: see TEPPANYAKI chapter, page 222, for additional information on beef service):

Marbled choice	*Shimofuri sukiyaki* 霜降り肉のすき焼き
Prime filet	*Hi-re sukiyaki* ヒレ肉のすき焼き
"Roast" regular cut	*Roosu sukiyaki* ロース肉のすき焼き

Since *sukiyaki* and *shabu-shabu* restaurants are derived from the Western custom of eating meat, course meals, graded alphabetically "A, B or C" (*ei koosu*, *bii koosu*, *shii koosu*) have always been the normal way for Japanese to order. However, ranking by poetic names or by the system of *nami* (regular), *jo* (choice) and tokujo (special) can also be found.

A La Carte Sukiyaki Menu

A la carte items often include the following:

Beef *sashimi*	*Gyuu sashi* 牛刺し
Crab (Alaskan king)	*Taraba-gani* たらばがに
Crab *tempura*	*Kani no tempura* かにの天ぷら
Creamed chicken	*Wakadori no kuri-imuni* 若鳥のクリーム煮
Smoked salmon	*Sumooku saamon* スモーク・サーモン
Tempura course meal	*Tempura teishoku* 天ぷら定食
Udon sukiyaki (stew of udon noodles, crab, scallops, fresh vegetables)	*Udonsuki* うどんすき

Unlike most Japanese restaurants, where wine is not available, at *sukiyaki* and *shabu-shabu* restaurants, wine is normally ordered with the meal, in addition to the regular fare of beer, *sake*, whiskey and soft drinks.

●

SHABU-SHABU

To many, *shabu-shabu* is another word for ambrosia, unrivalled for its succulent paper-thin folds of moist, tender beef (see color photo on page 155). Fabled abroad as a "Japanese fondue," *shabu-shabu* was created after WWII by a Kyoto cook, who got a hint for the new cooking-style from China and the donut-shapped Mongolian hot-pot (*hokonabe*). The name *shabu-shabu* in Japanese is onomatopoeic for the sound made by swishing one's meat in the boiling broth.

As in *sukiyaki* cooking, customers sit around a table with a gas burner in the center and share cooking duties. The waitress will bring a platter of prepared ingredients and a platter of marbled beef slices decoratively arranged. She will light the burner, set a hunk of *kombu* kelp into the hot-pot to flavor the broth, and aside from coming back to skim foam off the top from time to time, will leave the customers to their own devices.

Dunk and hold the meat in the broth for a few seconds and it will be done. Be careful not to let go; after all, someone else might latch onto your tasty morsel. Dip it in the toasted ground white sesame sauce with diced green onions and enjoy! Vegetables should be dropped in the boiling water and retrieved later. They go best with the *ponzu*, or sour sauce of bitter oranges. If you want more ingredients, ask your waitress. *Shabu-shabu* fans drink *sake*, cold beer (*biiru*), hot green tea (*ocha*) or a dry red wine (wain) with their repast.

To cap off the meal, the restaurant will probably bring flat *kishimen* noodles in the broth or simply serve the broth as a final soup in a bowl brought by the waitress, to be drunk after being lightly seasoned with diced green onions. For dessert (service catering to Westerners), green tea ice cream (*matcha* aisu kuriimu) is often available, so anyone whose meat got side-swiped from the hot-pot might want to recoup with a dish!

Recommended Restaurants

Type of Food	Zone	Restaurant Name	Map-Rest. No.	Floor
Shabu-shabu	Akasaka	☆ KISOJI	1–18	2F
Shabu-shabu	Akasaka	☆ EDOGYU	2–7	2F
Shabu-shabu	Ginza	☆ BANBAN-TEI	7–1	B1
Shabu-shabu	Ginza	☆ KAKIYASU	7–9	4F
Shabu-shabu	Ginza	☆ TAKAO	8–24	8F
Shabu-shabu	Ginza	☆ SHABUSEN	13–6	B2
Shabu-shabu	Ginza	☆ SHABUSEN	13–7	2F
Shabu-shabu	Ginza	☆ MIKASAKAIKAN	13–13	1F
Shabu-shabu	Ginza	☆ HIIRAGI	14–12	B1
Shabu-shabu	Roppongi	☆ CHAKO	20–9	3F
Shabu-shabu	Roppongi	☆ HASSAN	20–26	B1
Shabu-shabu	Roppongi	☆ SERYNA	21–6	1F
Shabu-shabu	Shinjuku	☆ SANRIBA	29–7	50F
Shabu-shabu	Shinjuku	☆ SERYNA	29–8	52F
Sukiyaki	Asakusa	☆ CHIN-YA	5–13	1F
Sukiyaki	Asakusa	☆ IMAHAN HONTEN	5–15	1F
Sukiyaki	Ginza	☆ KOKONOE	8–23	1F
Sukiyaki	Ginza	☆ OKAHAN	14–5	7F
Sukiyaki	Ginza	☆ WARAKU	15–23	1F
Sukiyaki	Nihombashi	☆ AO-I	16–3	1F
Sukiyaki	Nihombashi	☆ ZAKURO	17–11	B1
Sukiyaki	Shinjuku	☆ OKAHAN	29–19	7F
Sukiyaki	Shinjuku	☆ KOBAYASHI	32–3	1F

● Steak Grills:
Teppanyaki

Teppanyaki, the style of preparing and cooking food on a hot table-top grill, represents the marriage of Japanese sword-play to meat-eating (see color photo on page 156). In the Japanese restaurant near Boston where I once worked, the *teppanyaki* chef used to do terrifying behind-the back tosses of his cutting knife and could play jazz with the pepper shakers. With the clickety-clack of his spatula and knife, he would ricochet shrimp tails or steak morsels to each customer's plate, as they sat entranced by his magical tableside manner.

Just as American-style pizza is alien to Italy, in Japan, the famous American *teppanyaki* steak chain "Benihana of Tokyo" advertizes itself as "Benihana of New York".

Nonetheless, *teppanyaki* is an apt member of the Japanese family of foods. It celebrates the virtuosity of the Japanese chef's knife with the reverence a *samurai* might accord his sword.

●
History of Teppanyaki

The single-edged Japanese cutting knife, or *hocho* is more than just a cooking utensil. It embodies the cook's character. Unlike a restaurant's pots and pans, knives are a Japanese cook's private possessions which he will carry with him to whatever establishment he may be employed.

Forged of the same subtle combination of soft iron and hard steel as the Japanese sword, *hocho* offer the right amount of friction between blade and food so that even the most delicate raw fish, for instance, preserves razor sharp contours after being cut. Indeed, electron microscope analysis of the cells on the cut surfaces of food indicate the superiority and precision of the *hocho's* cutting edge.

In Japanese, a chef is called an *itamae* or "one who stands before a cutting board." Cutting is the primary task of the cook, since Japanese food does not rely on sauces, but rather emphasizes the natural flavors of ingredients. It is no wonder, therefore, that *teppanyaki*, in which the cook has an opportunity to show off his skill in slicing and arranging food, has achieved the stature in the West of the premier Japanese cuisine: although in Japan, it is a postwar invention stemming from *okonomiyaki* griddle-cooking. (See **OKONOMIYAKI** chapter, page 135)

●

Recognizing a Teppanyaki Restaurant

Teppanyaki restaurants can be spotted by their "ranch-style Japanese" architecture, whose decorative dark cross beams and white plaster walls are reminiscent of a Swiss mountain farmhouse or chalet. The decor is meant to evoke a feeling of the frontier atmosphere of Japan's farming wilderness on the northern island of Hokkaido, which is famous for its dairy products and where many of Japan's cattle are raised.

Atmosphere and Service

As steak restaurants, *teppanyaki* establishments have a Western atmosphere, often including a bar, though some are decorated with folkcrafts. The chef wears a tall, puffy cook's hat and stands facing six to ten customers around the counter of his grill top. He serves them straight from the grill. Unlike its poor cousin, *okonomiyaki*, *teppanyaki* provides a continental European dining atmosphere. *Teppanyaki* is best enjoyed with a bottle of wine or Japan's hearty draft beer that is usually available from April to September.

Gourmet Tips

The chef will ask you how you would like your meat done. The words "rare, medium and well-done" can be used in Japan if pronounced "properly" as *reaa* (レア), *midiamu* (ミディアム) and *uerudan* (ウエルダン).

Sauces are provided for each of the items served: a sesame mixture for seafood, lusty soy sauce and grated radish mixture for beef and so forth. Some restaurants boast that they grind their own sesame seed sauce, as is true of *tonkatsu* pork cutlet establishments.

Ordering from the Teppanyaki Menu

The ingredients for *teppanyaki* are brought by the chef to the table in prepared batches, as in *okonomiyaki*.

Sirloin	Saaroin suteeki サーロイン・ステーキ
Tenderloin	Tendaroin suteeki テンダーロイン・ステーキ

Steak Weight Converter

Steak is usually specified by weight, starting at 200 grams and increasing in increments of 50 grams. (A quarter pound steak is equivalent to 113.4 grams).

Pounds	Grams
0.44 lb	200 gm (nihyaku guramu)
½ lb	250 gm (nihyaku-goju guramu)
0.66 lb	300 gm (sambyaku guramu)
¾ lb	350 gm (sambyaku-goju guramu)
0.88 lb	400 gm (yonhyaku guramu)
1.10 lbs	500 gm (gohyaku guramu)

Teppanyaki Grilling Styles

The choice of grilling styles may include the following:

Regular	*Teppanyaki, futsuu* 鉄板焼き（普通）
In butter	*Bataa-yaki* バター焼き
In sherry	*Sherii-yaki* シェリー焼き
On a wire grill	*Ami-yaki* 網焼き

A La Carte Teppanyaki Menu

Generally, there is also a choice of a chicken, seafood (particularly squid, scallops or abalone), pork, liver or a vegetable course; however, these items can also be ordered *à la carte*.

MEATS & SEAFOODS

Abalone	*Awabi* あわび
Chicken	*Tori* 鳥

Crab	*Kani* かに
Liver	*Rebaa* レバー
Lobster	*Ise-ebi* 伊勢えび
Pork	*Buta* 豚
Scallops	*Hotategai* ほたて貝
Shrimp	*Ebi* えび
Squid	*Ika* いか

VEGETABLES

Champignon	*Mashuruumu* マッシュルーム
Mushrooms (slender)	*Shimeji* しめじ
Seasonal vegetables	*Kisetsu no yasai* 季節の野菜
Snow peas	*Saya-endo* さやえんどう

Japanese style course meals (*wa-teishoku*) are graded by the weight of the sirloin filet or Kobe beef being prepared, and given various names by the restaurant. For ordering, you should not be concerned about translating such fanciful names. Simply order according to your budget.

Steak Grills *Teppanyaki*

Recommended Restaurants

Type of Food	Zone	Restaurant Name	Map-Rest. No.	Floor
Teppanyaki	Akasaka	KANGETSU	1–22	B1
Teppanyaki	Ginza	BIIDORO-TEI	9–4	3F
Teppanyaki	Ginza	BENIHANA	12–13	1F
Teppanyaki	Ginza	☆ BENKEI	14–1	2F
Teppanyaki	Roppongi	☆ KORUZA	20–21	B1
Teppanyaki	Roppongi	KOBE 77	20–28	B1
Teppanyaki	Shinjuku	TONKICHI	34–4	B1

● Fresh Seafood Cuisine:
Sushi and Sashimi

As addictively delicious as a sweet slab of filet mignon, one that melts in your mouth, that's *sushi*! Few food enthusiasts anywhere in the world need be reminded what its ingredient are: a bite-sized mound of vinegared rice, a dab of zesty *wasabi* horseradish and, a slice of choice raw (and odorless!) seafood. Although this recipe may sound simple, every facet of making *sushi* demands specialized knowledge. Indeed, there is perhaps no more luxurious form of food in the world, considering that each mouthful is a prime morsel of fresh fish, individually selected, cut and catered by an expert with over 10 years of experience (see color photo on page 158). And only in Japan can such *sushi* expertise be savored to the full.

●
History of Sushi

Originally, the word *sushi* referred to any food including fish preserved by being placed between two layers of cooked rice. When the rice fermented and became sour, the fish acquired a delicate tangy flavor. This method of pickling was used for preserving meats in the 8th century, *nare-zushi* for example. Today this type of *sushi*, in which the rice is used to pickle but is not eaten, can still be found around Lake Biwa near Kyoto, served in the well-known dish, *funa-zushi* (carp *sushi*).

Later in history, the preservative power of vinegar, the *su* of *sushi*, was harnessed by mixing vinegar with freshly cooked rice. In the Edo period (1603–1868) *sushi* became popular among *kabuki* theater viewers because of its convenient bite-sized form, which was ideally suited for a lunchbox for a long, hungry day spent in a theater.

Recognizing a Sushi Restaurant

A *sushi* restaurant is easy to locate thanks to its Japanese exterior and traditionally lettered sign, or else by its navy blue *noren* cloth door-curtains. Look for the single-stroke *shi* (し) of *sushi* (寿し), as it is often extended the length of the sign along with the distinctive octopus-like character for *su*.

Atmosphere and Service

The typical street-corner *sushi* restaurant has a long white cyprus counter for customers to sit at, and on which the *sushi* is often directly served. In front of them is a refrigerated glass showcase where fillets of fish and an assortment of shellfish and seaweed is stacked.

Eating *sushi* is an educational experience which teaches the diner the taste of dozens of varieties of fresh fish. Yet it is also a talent show. The *sushi* chef,

Fresh
Seafood Cuisines

*Sushi
Sashimi*

wearing his white frock and with a *hachimaki* towel wrapped rakishly around his head, enjoys establishing a rapport with his customers. He also enjoys exhibiting his knifework and two-fingered rice-ball patting technique, with the ceremony and skill due to years of non-stop, seven-day-a-week apprenticeship.

▲ *Sushi* counter service

●
Gourmet Tips

Sushi restaurants take care to choose fish in season since freshness is essential to flavor and texture. Various factors, such as sea current, and spawning times determine when fish may best be caught and when they have a flavorsome oil content. Various kinds of tuna, bream, and mackerel are available year round. The winter months are best for savoring *hon-maguro* (a tuna that many consider the finest—fatty bellied yellowtail), *sawara* mackerel, and tiny whitebait (*shirauo*) which are brought to the table still leaping. From April through June, try Japan's king of saltwater fish, sea bream (*tai*), as well as *karei* flounder, its great rival in popularity. Firm, distinctive bonito (*katsuo*) *sashimi* is fresh as a spring day, and "dancing" shrimp (*ebi o-dori*) take us into the first hot days of the year. High summer is marked by dishes featuring the king of fresh-water fish, carp (*koi*), as well as by perch (*aodai*) and *anago* or *hamo* sea eel. And who could possibly mourn the passing year considering that as autumn comes, mackerel, various bream and clams becomes available, and that when the winter cold sets in, oysters, and *hirame* flounder are yours to feast upon. If you want the fish which is in season, just say *shun no sakana o kudasai*.

Rice balls also require expertise, and it is even said that all of the some 300 grains of rice should line up in the same direction if the chef properly nurses them in his palm. The rice, both plain and boiled, is a little harder and "chewier" that normal rice since it is tossed in a shallow wooden tub with hot water and, after being cooked in less water than normal, cooled in thin layers.

In Tokyo, go to Tsukiji, the location of the world's largest fish market, where some 600 of the 3,300 varieties of fish caught off the island waters of Japan are available daily. It's a beehive of activity since every morning an incredible 3,500 tons of fish pass hands in the space of three to four hours. In general, it is said that Japanese prefer fish from the sea to freshwater varieties.

Sushi is such a different experience that frankly, even if you have eaten a certain fish cooked (like tunafish), you will find the *sushi* version (*maguro* or *toro*) totally new and delicious. There is a LIST OF JAPANESE FISH

AND SEAFOOD NAMES at the end of this chapter. Use it, not as a checklist of what to eat, but rather as a vocabulary list for telling your fellow diners about your favorite *sushi* dishes.

Sushi should be eaten with chopsticks, or one's fingers, by turning it upside down and brushing a bit of soy sauce on the fish. Immersing the rice in the sauce will cause the whole mass to disintegrate. The slices of ginger, and cup of tea that go with *sushi* are provided to refresh the mouth so that you can really taste each bite. An *oshibori*, or damp handtowel, serves to keep one's fingers from getting sticky with the rice.

Sushi shops have their own specialized vocabulary. If you use *sushi* argot, you can easily gain the chef's appreciation and the type of service fit for a gourmet.

	Sushi Argot	Literal Meaning	Japanese
Chopsticks	*Otemoto*	By one's fingertips	*Hashi*
Horseradish	*Namida*	Tears	*Wasabi*
Salt	*Namino hana*	Flower of the waves	*Shio*
Soy sauce	*Murasaki*	Purple	*Shoyu*
Tea	*Agari*	The end	*Ocha*
Vinegared ginger	*Gari*	Foraged	*Sushoga*

●
Ordering from the Sushi Menu

Sushi can be enjoyed in any sequence since you select it from the display case in front of your eyes. However, some claim that the classical order for eating *sushi* is in a six-step cycle beginning with red, then white and finally blue: *maguro* tuna, white-meat fish (such as *hirame* flounder), *ika* squid, blue-meat fish (such as *saba* mackerel), cooked fish (such as sea eel *anago*), and one's personal favorite—from soft *uni* sea-urchin roe to firm *ebi* prawn or crunchy *awabi* abalone.

▲ Tokyo-style *sushi* on rice (*Nigiri-zushi*)

▲ *Chirashi-zushi* and *Tekka-don*

Fresh
Seafood Cuisines

*Sushi
Sashimi*

69

▶ Rice in
tofu pouch
(*Inari-zushi*)

Standard Sushi Dishes

Standard sushi dishes found at most sushi restaurants
are as follows:

Nigiri-zushi にぎりずし
Another word for *sushi* is *nigiri-zushi*, so-called for the
method of "squeezing" the rice balls into oblong bite-
sized balls. Typically, a *setto* (set) consists of seven rice
"fingers" convered with *maguro* tuna, *tai* sea bream,
ika cuttlefish, *akagai* ark-shell, *tako* octopus, *ebi* prawn
and *tamago* or layer-fried omlette.

Chirashi-zushi ちらしずし
Literally "scattered" *sushi*, consisting of a selection of
raw fish arranged attractively atop rice served in a
lacquered container.

Tekka-don 鉄火丼
Slices of red tuna *maguro* on rice in a lacquered container.

Gomoku-zushi 五目ずし
Mixed *sushi*, literally "five-items" sushi

Maki-zushi 巻きずし
A la carte service of narrow strips of seafood, crisp vegetables *yasai* vegetables, *natto* fermented soybeans or *tsukemono* pickles, are rolled with rice inside a sheet of crunchy, toasted *nori* seaweed.

Kappa-maki かっぱ巻き
A type of *maki-zushi* consisting of rice and cucumbers rolled in dried *nori* seaweed.

Inari-zushi いなりずし
A filling combination of vinegard rice and chopped vegetables stuffed into a pouch of fried *tofu* bean curd called *abura-age*, which legend has it is a favorite of foxes and women, who are patronized by the Shinto god, *Inari*. The *abura-age* bags are often tied with a *kampyo* gourd sliver.

●
SASHIMI

Sashimi, or literally the "sliced flesh" of raw fish without any rice, may at first seem an unbearably exotic, even barbaric, dish to foreigners. Yet in South America, *seviché*, or raw fish eaten with lemon juice, is a popular delicacy. Again, in the West, raw cherrystone clams and oysters, not to mention steak *tartar* and extra rare roast beef are common, so the odorless and succulent meat of flipping fresh fish ought rightly to be welcomed into the ranks of haute cuisine. *Sashimi* is prized not as a meal, but rather as a delectable hors d'oeuvre akin to a fine *pâté* or filet mignon appetizer (see color photo on page 159). It goes along with *sake* at parties and banquets, or with *tempura*, eel and *nabemono* meals.

Sashimi is eaten with chopsticks, being dipped into a low dish containing a specially prepared *sashimi* soy sauce mixture into which one should mix the light green cone of *wasabi* horseradish found in one's *sashimi* bowl. The soy sauce is spiced occasionally with grated ginger *gari* which serves the same purpose of freshening one's mouth as *wasabi* horseradish.

●

Styles of Sashimi Preparation

Sashimi 刺し身
Plain raw fish without rice. Five or six one-half inch thick rectangular slices come arranged like fallen dominoes either in a bowl or on a wooden tray. Other garnishes *(tsuma)* which add color are carrots, cucumbers, chrysanthemum flowers (bitter but edible!) and *shiso* which is a delicious leaf blending the flavors of lemon and mint. Another popular way of serving *sashimi* is in paper-thin slices arranged in a rosette pattern on a platter. The sauce in this case is a tangy mixture of citrus and soy sauce called *ponzu*.

Tataki たたき
Literally "pounded," refers to *sashimi* with its outer meat softened either by light mincing of the surface, or more commonly, brazing over a charcoal fire before being sliced. *Katsuo* skipjack is a favorite served this way.

Arai あらい
Arai is a type of *sashimi* especially served during the hot summer season. *Tai* bream or *koi* carp slices are placed on a dish, and hot water is then poured over them until the outsides turn white and the slices curl up.

Ikizukuri 活き作り
Ikizukuri or literally "live masterpiece" requires the

highest skill in preparing raw fish. A live fish is selected from the restaurant's fish tank; in some restaurants, the diner himself makes the selection. The chef then prepares it by slicing the meat off one side of the backbone. The *sashimi* is then placed amongst a seaweed garnish and carefully arranged against the carcass which still trembling is set bowed as if it magically jumped out of the water and onto your plate. *Ikizukuri* is without a doubt the chef d'oeuvre of freshness.

▲ Sculptured fish display (*Ikizukuri*)

Fresh
Seafood Cuisines
*Sushi.
Sashimi.*

Recommended Restaurants

Type of Food	Zone	Restaurant Name	Map-Rest. No.	Floor
Sushi	Akasaka	☆ KINPA	3–12	B1
Sushi	Asakusa	☆ SUSHIYOSHI	4–10	1F
Sushi	Asakusa	☆ SUSHIHATSU	4–11	1F
Sushi	Asakusa	☆ KIBUN-ZUSHI	5–9	1F
Sushi	Ginza	☆ YACHIYO	7–5	1F
Sushi	Ginza	☆ HATSUNE-ZUSHI	9–1	1F
Sushi	Ginza	☆ FUKUSUKE	10–3	8F
Sushi	Ginza	☆ KAMPACHI	12–28	1F
Sushi	Ginza	☆ AO-YAGI	13–11	1F
Sushi	Ginza	☆ SUSHIKO	14–8	1F
Sushi	Ginza	☆ UO-MASA	14–16	1F
Sushi	Ginza	☆ SUSHIKIYO	15–9	5F
Sushi	Nihombashi	☆ EIRAKU-ZUSHI	16–5	1F
Sushi	Nihombashi	☆ YOSHINO-ZUSHI	17–13	1F
Sushi	Nihombashi	☆ YOSHINO	17–16	B1
Sushi	Nihombashi	☆ SUSHITETSU	18–8	2F
Sushi	Nihombashi	☆ SUSHI-KYU	18–10	B1
Sushi	Nihombashi	☆ HATSUNE-ZUSHI	18–13	1F
Sushi	Roppongi	☆ OTSUNA-ZUSHI	20–13	B1
Sushi	Roppongi	☆ OTSUNA-ZUSHI	20–16	1F
Sushi	Roppongi	☆ ZOROKU-ZUSHI	21–5	1F
Sushi	Shibuya	☆ SUSHIFUMI	24–14	1F
Sushi	Shibuya	☆ YANAGI-ZUSHI	24–19	1F
Sushi	Shinjuku	☆ SUSHITA	29–13	B1
Sushi	Shinjuku	☆ KYUBE	29–16	7F
Sushi	Shinjuku	☆ TAMAGAWA-ZUSHI	35–2	1F
Sushi	Shinjuku	☆ KYOCHA-YA	35–18	B1
Sushi	Tsukiji	☆ EDOGIN	36–1	1F
Sushi	Tsukiji	☆ CHIKARA-ZUSHI	36–2	1F
Sushi	Tsukiji	☆ SUSHI-IWA	36–6	1F
Sushi	Tsukiji	☆ SUSHISEI	36–7	1F
Sushi	Tsukiji	☆ KIRAKU-ZUSHI	36–8	1F
Sushi	Tsukiji	☆ TAMA-ZUSHI HONTEN	37–5	1F
Ikizukuri	Ginza	☆ MIKAZUKI-TEI	15–19	1F
Ikizukuri	Ueno	☆ SANTOMO	38–2	1F
Kani	Akasaka	☆ KANIDORAKU	3–16	1F
Kani	Ginza	☆ KANISEN	13–24	1F
Kani	Shibuya	☆ KANI-YA	22–29	B1
Kani	Shibuya	☆ KANITANI	24–7	8F
Kani	Ueno	KANI-YA HONTEN	38–8	1F
Kani/niku-ryori	Roppongi	☆ DAIKAN-KAMADO	20–17	1F
Kani/niku-ryori	Roppongi	☆ FOX-TAIL	21–9	B1

List of Japanese Fish and Seafood Names

Asterisks * indicate most commonly served seafood.
Numbers in the list indicate one of the following
seafood categories other than fish.

Seafood Categories Other Than Fish	
1. Crab	5. Shrimp
2. Shellfish	6. Squid and
3. Caviar	Octopus
4. Eel	7. Others

Ainame		Fat cod/greenling
* *Akagai*	2	Ark shell
* *Amadai*		Blanquillos/tile fish
* *Anago*	4	Sea eel/conger eel
Anko		Angler fish/frogfish
Aodai		Blue fusilier
Aoyagi	2	Trough shell
* *Asari*	2	Short-necked clam
* *Awabi*	2	Abalone
* *Ayu*		Japanese samlet/sweet smelt
Bakagai	2	Trough shell
Beni-masu		Red salmon
* *Bora*		Grey mullet
* *Buri*		Yellowtail (adult)
* *Dojo*		Loach
Donko		Sleeper/goby
Dorome		Gluttonous goby
E-i		Stingray
* *Ebi*	5	Shrimp (general)
Eso		Lizard fish
* *Fugu*		Globefish/pufferfish/blowfish

Fresh
Seafood Cuisines

*Sushi
Sashimi*

* Fuka		Shark
* Funa		Crucian carp
Gimpo		Gunnel
Ha-gatsuo		Belted bonito
* Hamachi		Yellowtail (pre-adult)
Hamadai		Ruby Snapper
* Hamaguri	2	Asiatic hard shell clam
* Hamo	4	Sharp-toothed eel
Hata		Grouper
* Hatahata		Sailfin sandfish
* Haze		Goby
Hira		Long-finned herring
* Hirame		Flounder/flatfish
Hobo		Bluefin sea robin/gurnard
* Hokke		Atka-mackerel
Hokkigai	2	Surf clam
* Hotategai	2	Scallop
* Hoya	2	Sea squirt/ascidian
Igai	2	Hard-shelled mussel
Ii-dako	6	Octopus (tiny)
* Ika	6	Squid/cuttlefish (general)
* Ikanago	4	Sand lance
* Ikura	3	Salted caviar/salmon roe
* Isaki		Grunt
* Ise-ebi	5	Spiny lobster
Ishidai		Parrot fish
Ishimochi		Croaker
* Iwana		Char
* Iwashi		Sardine
* Kaibashira	2	Scallop centers
Kajiki		Swordfish/marlin
* Kaki	2	Oyster
* Kamasu		Pike/pacific barracuda
* Kani	1	Crab (general)
Karasugai	2	Freshwater mussel
Karasugarei		Greenland halibut

* Karei		Halibut/flatfish
* Katakuchi-iwashi		Anchovy
* Katsuo		Bonito/skipjack tuna
Kawa-gani	1	River crab
* Kazunoko	3	Herring roe
Ke-gani	1	Crab
* Kibinago		Blue sprat
Kidai		Yellow porgy
* Kisu		Sillago/smelt
* Ko-ika	6	Small cuttlefish
Kochi		Flathead
* Kohada		Gizzard shad (med. size)
* Koi		Carp
Konoshiro		Gizzard shad (large size)
Korai-ebi	5	Yellow sea prawn
* Kujira	7	Whale
* Kurage		Jellyfish
Kuro-dai		Black porgy
Kuro-maguro		Blue-fin tuna/tunny
* Kuruma-ebi	5	Prawn
Ma-aji		Horse mackerel/saurel
Ma-iwashi		True sardine/pilchard
Madai		Genuine porgy/red sea bream
Madara		Pacific cod/Alaskan codfish
Magarei		Brown sole
* Maguro		Tuna
Makajiki		Striped marlin
Managatsuo		Harvest fish
* Masu		Trout
Mebachi		Bigeye tuna
* Mebaru		Black rockfish/Japanese stingfish
Megochi		Flathead
Mekajiki		Swordfish/broadbill
* Menuke		Matsubara stingfish
Mirugai	2	Surf clam

Mongo-ika	6	Cuttlefish
Muro-aji		Horse-scad mackerel/scad
Mutsu		Bluefish
Mutsugoro		Blue-spotted mud hopper
* *Namako*	7	Sea cucumber/trepang/ *bêche-de-mer*
* *Namazu*		Catfish/mudfish
Nijimasu		Rainbow trout
* *Nishin*		Pacific Herring
Ohyo		Pacific halibut
Okoze		Stonefish/lumpfish
Sa-me		Shark
* *Saba*		Mackerel
* *Sake*		Salmon
Sakura-ebi	5	Cocktail shrimp
* *Samma*		Pacific saury
Sawa-gani	1	Freshwater crab
* *Sawara*		Spanish mackerel
* *Sayori*		Halfbeak/needlefish
* *Saza-e*	2	Conch shell/turbo
* *Shako*	5	Mantis shrimp/squilla
* *Shiba-ebi*	5	Prawn
* *Shijimi*	2	Corbicula
Shima-aji		Striped jack
* *Shira-uo*		Whitefish/icefish
* *Shishamo*		Shishamo smelt/capelin
Shitabirame		Sole
Sujiko	3	Salmon roe
Suketodara		Alaskan pollock
* *Surume-ika*	6	Sagittated calamary
* *Suzuki*		Sea bass
* *Tachi-uo*		Hairtail/cutlass fish
* *Tai*		Sea bream
Tairagi	2	Razor shell/fan shell
Taisho-ebi	5	Prawn
Takabe		Yellowstriped butterfish

* *Tako*	6	Octopus
Tanago		Sea chub
* *Tanishi*	2	Pond snail
* *Tara*		Cod
* *Taraba-gani*	1	King crab
* *Tarako*	3	Cod roe
* *Tobi-uo*		Flying fish
Tokobushi	2	Abalone (small)
* *Torigai*	2	Cockle
* *Toro*		Tuna (belly)
* *Ubagai*	2	Surf clam
* *Umitake*	2	Clam/barnea dilatata
* *Unagi*	4	Eel
* *Uni*	2	Sea urchin
* *Wakasagi*		Pond smelt
Warasa		Yellowtail (pre-adult)
Watari-gani	1	Blue crab

● Pufferfish Cuisine:
Fugu

If you view eating pufferfish as a form of Russian roulette, you may be surprised to learn that the "gun" is never loaded. The pufferfish used in the Japanese cuisine is a special variety (mainly *tora fugu*) which has negligible amounts of toxins. Moreover, the pufferfish, better known by its Japanese name, *fugu*, is a delicacy.

The raw meat is sliced paper thin and arranged artistically in rosettes that reveal the pattern of the dish it is presented on (see color photo on page 161). Whether dipped in the piquant soy, chive and bitter orange sauce or eaten as chowder, or with rice porridge, the *fugu* has a delicious taste. The large number of *fugu* restaurants in Tokyo attests to the fact that its pearly white meat attracts and makes addicts of many a gourmet.

▲ Pufferfish

History of Fugu

Eating *fugu* developed in Kyushu where the best edible kinds are found in abundance during the winter months. The name *fugu* comes from *fuku* (to swell) as in the Japanese proverb about people who internalize their worries: "If you don't speak (about your problems), your stomach swells."

Because of its small fins, the *fugu* is a very slow-moving, comical looking fish, which has evolved the peculiar defense mechanism of inhaling water into its stomach so as to turn its appetizing looking body into a menacing ball twice its normal size. This characteristic led the Japanese to spell *fugu* with the Chinese characters for "riverpig" (although it is a salt-water fish), and gave it the English names, balloonfish, pufferfish, swellfish, blowfish and globefish.

Served only in wintertime to avoid increased toxic levels generated as a reproductive defense mechanism, *fugu* cuisine is regulated by Japanese law and can only be served by licensed chefs to ensure that the proper varieties are used.

Recognizing a Fugu Restaurant

The some 30 *fugu* specialty restaurants and 2,000 other licensed establishments in Tokyo serving *fugu* are easy to recognize thanks to the *fugu*'s balloon shape. Spherical lanterns of the *fugu*'s preserved hide, clay replicas, a noren curtain or a lantern bearing their resemblance hang out front as a beacon to the *fugu* lover.

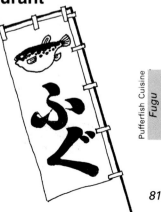

Pufferfish Cuisine
Fugu

81

Atmosphere and Service

Although specialty fugu restaurants are open, at most, 171 days a year in the wintertime, they still provide an amazing amount of personal attention. Often the *fugu-ya* is a small family business. Enjoy watching the chef slice the fillets paper thin and make them into a decorative display.

▲ Pufferfish service

◀ Pufferfish restaurant front

Gourmet Tips

Fugu meat is a cross between crunchy and chewy, said by the Japanese to go *shiko shiko* in one's mouth when absolutely fresh. The best restaurants have it brought by the blue "bullet" train all the way from Shimonoseki (said to be the best source) on the Western tip of the main Japanese island of Honshu, bordering Kyushu. Since December, January and February are the months *fugu* is in season another specialty offered by many *fugu* restaurants is *nabe*. (See the chapter on **NABE-MONO**, page 109.)

●

Ordering from the Fugu Menu

Fugu menus are predictable although most restaurants have their own specialty. A course meal consists of:

The Fugu Course Meal

Fugu-sashi ふぐ刺し
sliced raw pufferfish eaten with *ponzu* sauce—soy sauce juice of Japan's native bitter orange and green chives.

Fuguchiri ふぐちり
Literally, "shredded *fugu*" tossed into a rich vegetable chowder—perfect on a winter day

Fuguzosui ふぐ雑炊
A rice porridge flavored with the broth from *fugu* cooking.

Mizutaki 水炊き
A tableside boiling broth dip (merely boiled *fugu*) served instead of *zosui*

Hirezake ひれ酒
Although most Westerners can't stand the strong fishy taste, toasted fugu fins are dunked in hot sake, and eaten by the hearty zealot as a crisp *digestive*

Also, a restaurant may have *tempura*, sausage (*kamaboko*) or gellied consomme with tidbits (*nikogori* にこごり)—very haute cuisine.

Pufferfish Cuisine
Fugu

83

Other Foods at Fugu Restaurants

Most fugu establishments also carry other epicurean dishes, such as loaches (that is the English word, the Japanese word is *dojo* どじょう), angler fish (*anko* あんこう) which comes from the depth of the ocean floor, conch shell (or *sazae* さざえ), etc.

Recommended Restaurants

Type of Food	Zone	Restaurant Name	Map-Rest. No.	Floor
Fugu	Akasaka	☆ TAKIKAWA	3–19	1F
Fugu	Asakusa	☆ SANKAKU	5–11	1F
Fugu	Ginza	☆ GINICHI	15–1	2F
Fugu	Ginza	☆ NARUTO	15–14	1F
Fugu	Roppongi	☆ AJIMAN	21–10	1F
Fugu	Shibuya	☆ TSUKIJI	24–23	1F
Fugu/kani	Asakusa	☆ FUGUKAIKAN	5–6	1F
Fugu/kappo	Asakusa	☆ TSUKUMO	5–4	1F
Fugu/kappo	Shinjuku	☆ KIKUMI	29–12	B1
Fugu/kisetsu	Ginza	☆ TSUKIJI	12–11	B1
Fugu/nabe	Nihombashi	☆ HANKYO	16–2	B1
Fugu/nabe	Shibuya	☆ GIN-TEI	22–25	1F

● Barbecued Chicken Pubs:
Yakitori and Kushi-yaki

Japanese cooking rarely uses the oven, prefering instead the natural flavors directly imparted by the open flames of a grill and the personal attention of the chef. *Yakitori*, the method of basting chicken *(tori)* meat on tiny skewers in sweet soy sauce and grilling them over charcoal *(yaki)* is indeed primitive, yet the result is exquisite—meat crisp on the outside but tender and succulent inside. After one bite it is difficult not to become addicted and order platter after platter of *à la carte yakitori* delicacies (see color photo on page 162).

●
History of Yakitori

The Dutch living in Nagasaki are presumed to be the originators of the barbecued dish for which Tokyo is renowned today. Thus Nanbantei or literally "The Restaurant of the Southern Barbarians," is the name adopted by a *yakitori* chain located in Shibuya, Roppongi and Yurakucho.

●
Recognizing a Yakitori Restaurant

Every big station in Tokyo has a district full of *yakitori-ya* which you can recognize from the red lanterns or *aka-chochin* emblazoned with the character *tori* (鳥 or bird) hung outside. These so-called "red-lantern shops" sometimes employ men in white coats who stand in the street shouting a hearty welcome: *Sa.....irasshai!*

Many smaller shops advertise themselves by simply setting the narrow long charcoal braziers right out on the street. Some consist of a tiny cubicle with room for only five or six people, while more customers sit outside on overturned crates, or on stools.

● Atmosphere and Service

The true *yakitori* is a small eating establishment specializing in grilled chicken, and which in atmosphere, resembles a pub or small cafe in the West. Unlike a Japanese bar, cabaret, or nightclub, however, the *yakitori-ya* caters to the after-work crowd looking for an inexpensive drink, served along with tasty morsels of chicken and grilled vegetables.

Many of Japan's middle-aged white-collar workers (mainly men), frequent *yakitori-ya*. They'll have a beer or two and a light meal with fellow workers before catching a train home at the nearby station. With a family to feed on a meager salary, such customers can nonetheless rest assured that the bill will be small. A *yakitori-ya* is a place where only friends gather; there's no plush decor or music, just flavors from the grill and an uproar of conversation.

◀ Barbecued
chicken grill
(*Yakitori-ya*)

● Gourmet Tips

The smoke seen billowing from a shop is a welcome sign of genuine charcoal barbecuing. Connoisseurs insist that chicken must be cooked over charcoal made from the holm oak of Wakayama Prefecture, renowned the world over for its hardness. Though expensive, this *bincho* coal burns for eight hours. Yet many *yakitori-ya* use gas and electricity. Purists argue that gas gives off too much steam, leaving the chicken soggy, and that electricity is just not hot enough to broil the bird properly on the outside. The cook can be expected to dip the spit of meat or vegetables three times into the *tare* sometimes seasoned only with salt and hot pepper (in which case it is called *shioyaki*).

The more refined big brother of *yakitori* is *okariba-yaki*—which literally means "hunting food." This involves the cooking of poultry or game (in season) on steel plates over a gas or charcoal fire. It is served in an *o-zashiki* or traditional *tatami*-mat room.

Another popular chicken dish is *mizutaki* which consists of chicken stewed in a large earthenware pot on the table in front of you. An excellent chicken broth is left in the pot to finish up the meal.

● Ordering from the Yakitori Menu

Skewered and broiled over charcoal are cubes of chicken, often sandwiched on the same skewer between forest mushrooms, quail eggs, gingko nuts, slices of leeks, and savory sweet peppers. Also available are balls of chicken "meatballs," livers, wings, etc. Leg and thigh meat is usually tenderer than the fine-textured breast. Order what you fancy, and dip it in the soy-sugar-sauce provided. You pay for it by the stick.

A La Carte Yakitori Menu

(Note: asterisks * indicate recommended items)

OTSUMAMI (hors d'oeuvres)

Cold *tofu* with grated leek, ginger or skipjack	*Hiyayakko* 冷ややっこ
Cucumber with *miso* salad	*Morokyu* もろきゅう
Deep-fried chicken	*Kara-age* から揚げ
Grated yam with raw tuna	*Yamakake* 山かけ
Miso on raw tuna, seaweed	*Nuta* ぬた
Stew of pork tripe, potatoes, etc.	*Nikomi* 煮込み

CHICKEN

* Breast meat	*Sasami, yakitori* ささみ焼き鳥
Chicken and mushroom	*Shiitake toriyaki* しいたけ鳥焼き
Chicken and onion	*Negi toriyaki* ねぎ鳥焼き

Chicken and green peppers	*Piiman toriyaki* ピーマン鳥焼き
Giblets	*Motsu yaki* もつ焼き
Heart	*Hatsu yaki* ハツ焼き
Legs	*Momo yaki* もも焼き
* Liver	*Rebaa yaki* レバー焼き
* Meatballs	*Tsukune yaki* つくね焼き
Pope's nose	*Bonchiri yaki* ぽんちり焼き
* Skin	*Kawa yaki* 皮焼き
Tripe	*Shiro yaki* しろ焼き
* Wings	*Tebasaki yaki* 手羽先焼き

VEGETABLES

* Eggplants	*Nasu yaki* なす焼き
* Green peppers	*Piiman yaki* ピーマン焼き
* Mushrooms (oriental)	*Shiitake yaki* しいたけ焼き
Leeks	*Negi yaki* ねぎ焼き
Roasted gingko nuts	*Ginnan yaki* ぎんなん焼き
Vegetable combination	*Yasai yaki* 野菜焼き

OTHERS

| Duck | *Kamo yaki* かも焼き |
| Prawn | *Ebi yaki* えび焼き |

Barbecued
Chicken Pubs
Yakitori
Kushi-Yaki

Quail eggs	*Uzura yaki* うずら焼き
Scallops	*Hotate yaki* ほたて焼き
Sparrow	*Suzume yaki* すずめ焼き

In addition to these items, *yakitori-ya* serve other *o-tsumami* such as nabemono, oden, broiled fish, clams, and meat wrapped in *shiso* lemon-mint leaves as well as various salads, etc.

A companion treat to *yakitori* which is often offered by *yakitori-ya* in order to offer a filling meal is *kamameshi*, rice steamed in a special pot along with meat or shrimp, and vegetables. (See also the **KAMAMESHI** chapter, page 104.)

You might also try a charcoal broiled sparrow—its bones so light and crisp that you crush them in your mouth like you do the bones in canned salmon. Quail is also a popular dish in a *yakitori* shop.

Recommended Restaurants

Type of Food	Zone	Restaurant Name	Map-Rest. No.	Floor
Kushi-yaki	Shibuya	☆ KUSHINOBO	22–18	B1
Kushi-yaki	Shibuya	☆ HIDA TAKAYAMA	23–1	1F
Kushi-yaki	Shibuya	☆ ROWARU	23–2	1F
Kushi-yaki	Shibuya	☆ KUSHISUKE	24–4	B1
Tori-kappo	Shimbashi	☆ TORISHIGE	27–12	1F
Yakitori	Akasaka	☆ MARUKIN	1–16	1F
Yakitori	Ginza	☆ TORIMAN	15–16	1F
Yakitori	Nihombashi	☆ TOHACHI	19–5	B1
Yakitori	Roppongi	☆ KAMAKURA	20–18	B1
Yakitori	Roppongi	☆ NANBAN-TEI	21–1	1F
Yakitori	Roppongi	☆ KUSHIHACHI	21–3	3F
Yakitori	Shibuya	☆ NANBAN-TEI	23–4	2F
Yakitori	Shibuya	☆ SASAMEYUKI	24–16	1F
Yakitori	Shibuya	☆ NANBAN-TEI	26–14	1F

● Hearthside Grills:
Robatayaki

The warmth and chatter of an old-fashioned farm hearthplace best describes the *robatayaki* pub/restaurant. Welcomed with a hearty *irasshai* by the cooks, the visitor is ushered into a wood-shingled room decorated with dried preserves and straw raincoats hanging from the eaves.

Like sitting down to a smokeless, backyard charcoal grill, the customer can have the chef set abroiling any of the foods displayed banquet-style, and enjoy the savory smells over a mug of beer (see color photo on page 160). "Indoor Japanese barbecue" might explain the chef to you as he transfers a baked potato or grilled prawn to your plate from the *robata* burner, from which the restaurant derives its name.

●
History of Robatayaki

The *robata* around which all the activity centers at a *robatayaki* restaurant is the traditional Japanese living-room heating, toasting and pipe-lighting device. In an old-style Japanese house, there was a big square fireplace *(robata)* in the middle of the floor of a *tatami* room. A wooden pot hanger (*jizai*) was suspended over the *robata* to adjust the height of the pot over the flame. In the old days, people spent many hours during

Japan's cold months around the fireside, sharing the warmth of the fire. All the family members got together around the fireplace to enjoy the long winter evenings while reading, knitting, sewing and sometimes drinking sake or hot Japanese tea with their guests. The hearth at a farm was a four-by-four foot sunken fireplace in the middle of a large room. On the other hand, a tin *hibachi* set in an elegantly finished zelkova stand is what might have been used in a townhouse. Thus, at a high-class *robatayaki* restaurant, the townhouse variety, is found one to each private eight-mat room. But the pubs recreate the farmhouse. Even city Japanese can enjoy playing the "good old boy" around the hearth and home-cooking.

Recognizing a Robatayaki Restaurant

Robatayaki restaurants are common in the entertainment districts that men and women frequent after work and on weekends. The large red lanterns can be distinguished from the small ones hanging outside *yakitori* pubs by the small roofs sheltering them, or the box-like stands in which they're fitted. If there are no lanterns in sight, check for a rustic thatched-roof storefront.

Atmosphere and Service

The cooks wear *happi*-coats and the waitresses *kimonos*. After you make an order, no matter how faltering the pronunciation of the Japanese, out it will resound with vigor from the order-takers lips who immediately relay it to the chefs. At some restaurants, such as Inaka-ya in Roppongi and Akasaka, which is a favorite of foreigners, the cooks kneel on a platform in the center of the counter area, and hand customers their dishes on long-handled paddles (see cover photo). There, the entire staff repeats orders in a chorus of shouts, so the atmosphere has all the heartiness of a country festival and young men shouldering *omikoshi* shrines.

Gourmet Tips

After trying the recommended orders (see next section below), the true connoisseur should take the opportunity to experiment with some of Japan's typical hors d'oeuvres. Try *shiokara*, which tastes like anchovies, very salty, and is made of squid or sometimes, for the drink-lover, tripe; the bitter tripe are reminiscent of a touch of vinegar. *Tsukimi-natto*, egg on fermented soybeans, is gooey but hearty. Or, for the adventurous, crunch down a whole grilled smelt (*shishamo*).

Ordering from the Robatayaki Menu

Robatayaki menus are not standardized, and in fact, include everything eaten in Japan. In particular, many of the fish available in raw form at a *sushi* restaurant are available here deliciously charcoal grilled. (Refer to the LIST OF JAPANESE FISH AND SEAFOOD NAMES, page 75.) You can also look around and try to get the same dish as your neighbors by pointing and saying, *onaji mono o kudasai* ("Please may I have the same"). Because robatayaki are considered as much pubs (*izakaya*) as restaurants, at the top of most menus is the liquor list—beer, sake, whiskey, etc.

A meal might start off with a few *kushiyaki* skewers of vegetables, then move onto a buttery stewed meat and potato dish, *nikujaga*, and after a couple more beers, graduate into the fish course (grilled, of course) with a dagger-like mackerel pike. Also, try the *sashimi* of yellowtail, *hamachi* or *hiyayakko*—that icy cold slice of tofu with fluffy shavings of salty dried fish, *hijiki* pickled seaweed and carrot . . . The list goes on and on of typical (and we mean absolutely staple fare to the Japanese) delicacies.

A La Carte Robatayaki Menu

(Note: for ordering *yakitori* entrees at a *robatayaki* restaurant, refer to the YAKITORI chapter, page 200)

SEAFOOD

Bonito (brazed lightly on the outside)	*Katsuo no tataki* かつおのたたき
Bonito (with soybean paste)	*Katsuo no misozukeyaki* かつおのみそづけ焼き
Clam	*Hamaguri* はまぐり
Conch shell (served like escargot)	*Sazae no tsuboyaki* さざえのつぼ焼き
Cuttlefish, dried	*Surume* するめ
Flounder	*Karei* かれい
Herring	*Nishin no shioyaki* にしんの塩焼き
Mackerel	*Aji*, *Hokke* あじ, ほっけ
Pike	*Samma* さんま
Salmon	*Sake* 鮭
Scallops	*Hotategai* ほたて貝
Smelt	*Shishamo* ししゃも
Squid	*Ika* いか
Tuna	*Maguro no teriyaki* まぐろの照り焼き

VEGETABLES

Eggplant	*Nasu* なす
Gingko nuts	*Ginnan* ぎんなん
Leeks	*Negi* ねぎ
Mushrooms (oriental)	*Shiitake* しいたけ
Peppers (the really tiny ones)	*Piman or shishito* ピーマン，ししとう
Potato (served with butter)	*Jagabataa* じゃがバター

Ironically, the menu will often include a rice addenda, as if to suggest that without adding these items you wouldn't be stuffed already. But every Japanese needs his pickles, rice balls and tea to top off the meal. We recommend the grilled rice ball *(yaki-onigiri)*, an example of how good plain rice can taste. Other delicious items include:

Ochazuke お茶づけ
A bowl of rice "pickled" with hot green tea and either *umeboshi* (sour plum) or *sake* (salted salmon)

Gomoku kamameshi 五目かまめし
Rice casserole topped with chicken, vegetables, crab or shrimp, mushrooms, etc.

Robatayaki Broiling Techniques

In addition, *robatayaki* restaurants use other broiling techniques. Some of the major ones well worth inquiring about and trying are listed below.

Gimpaku-yaki 銀箔焼き
Ingredients are seasoned, wrapped in silver foil, and baked in an oven.

Horoku-yaki ほうろく焼き
Ingredients are arranged on a bed of salt in a special earthenware plate *(horoku)*, covered, and baked.

Kara-yaki 殻焼き
Shellfish baked in their shells.

Kimi-yaki 黄身焼き
Broiled food dipped in sweetened raw egg yolk.

Miso-yaki みそ焼き
Food, grilled and brushed with salty *miso* paste.

Namban-yaki 南蛮焼き
Broiled whole fish brushed with a mixture of chopped scallion and egg white.

Okariba-yaki お狩場焼き
Pan roasted poultry or game (literally, hunting food).

Shio-yaki 塩焼き
Fish sprinkled liberally with coarse salt, skewered and broiled.

Teri-yaki 照り焼き
Skewered ingredients are basted frequently with a sweetened soy sauce flavored with rice wine and grilled until they "shine".

Tsubo-yaki つぼ焼き
Shellfish grilled in its shell with seasonings, such as conch shell (turbo).

Uni-yaki うに焼き
Grilled food brushed with a paste made of sea urchin and egg yolk.

Recommended Restaurants

Type of Food	Zone	Restaurant Name	Map-Rest. No.	Floor
Robatayaki	Akasaka	☆ INAKA-YA	3–5	2F
Robatayaki	Shibuya	☆ TENGU	22–6	1F
Robatayaki	Shibuya	☆ FUNABENKEI	23–9	3F
Robatayaki	Shibuya	☆ INAKA	24–15	1F
Robatayaki	Shinjuku	☆ TARUGEN	29–10	49F
Robatayaki	Tsukiji	☆ HIDA	37–3	1F
Robatayaki	Ueno	☆ TARUMATSU	39–20	1F
Nishin-ryori	Shibuya	☆ ISOCHU	26–1	B1
Sakana	Roppongi	☆ CHIHEI	21–8	1F
Sakana	Shinjuku	☆ ISOHAMA	33–5	B1
Sakana/kani	Akasaka	☆ KAMADO-SHOGUN	1–3	B1
Sankai-ryori	Shibuya	☆ MICHINOKU	26–3	1F

● Broiled Eel Cuisine:
Unagi

Who would guess that eel can be made into a buttery brown fillet which is as rich and tender as pâté and deliciously melts in your mouth? (See color photo on page 161). No wonder then that one of the most popular foods among foreigners living in Japan is eel, or in Japanese, *unagi*. At a specialty eel restaurant, called an *unagi-ya*, fresh eel fillets are charcoal roasted on skewers, in combination with an intricate time-consuming marinating and steaming process. A full-course meal of eel is moderately expensive, but worth every month-watering inch.

●
History of Unagi

Perhaps because of the fact that *unagi* has more calories per gram than a sirloin steak, more vitamin-A even than carrots and many other vitamins as well, it is a popular health food to combat fatigue during the hot summer season. Tradition has it that *unagi* should be eaten as a "tonic" on the Day of the Ox (a lunar calendar day around July 20th), so that one can "become as strong as an ox." On that day, *unagi-ya* are always jam-packed. Some claim that the *samurai* inventor and writer, Hiraga Gennai started this custom during the Edo period in order to promote a friend's *unagi* restaurant business. Gennai placed a sign on the eel restaurant door, reading "*Ushi no Hi*" (The Day of the Ox), which supposedly baffled passersby into thinking that unagi was the holiday food which ought to be eaten on that particular day.

● Recognizing an Unagi Restaurant

Today's *unagi* restaurants are easy to spot because of distinctive vertical sign or flag, in which the Japanese letter "*u*" (う) of *unagi* (うなぎ) is elongated and two little fins are depicted near the letter's wriggling "head." The flags, generally one foot wide and four or five feet long, are flown vertically on a bamboo pole.

◀ Broiled eel restaurant front (*Unagi-ya*)

● Atmosphere and Service

There are usually both counters and tables available. *Unagi-ya* are generally small in scale, catering to a solid core of *unagi*-loving clientele, generally male. Because of the association by shape, *unagi* is reputed to improve virility, while the eye-like spots on the back of the *yatsume*, or "eight-eyed" eel, have fostered the belief that it helps improve one's eyesight, in the same way that the liver-shaped leaves of liverwort were believed to have medicinal properties in Medieval Europe.

Gourmet Tips

Unagi must be brought fresh to the restaurant, and kept there in tanks until preparation. In fact, it is not unusual to see a cook on his way back from the market, with a large plastic sack strapped onto the back of his bicycle in which the live eels are sloshing around. The true gourmet insists on wild eels, since meat of the cultivated eel is coarser and fattier. In Tokyo-style cooking, as opposed to that centering on Osaka, the fillet is steamed and rinsed after the first grilling to remove excess fat, prior to being coated with a fresh layer or sauce and grilled again. Thus there is never a hint of the muddy taste which characterizes eels prepared in the West. Both *hamo* and *anago* are species of sea eel which are delicious as *tempura*, or grilled and served in *sushi* with a sauce resembling *tare*.

Eels are difficult to catch. They can be bred, but only from larva caught on their way back to Japanese rivers from breeding grounds in the deepest reaches of the sea (some claim the Sargasso Sea). No wonder that *unagi* is a luxury to the Japanese, costing twice as much as an average "salaryman's" meal.

Ordering from the Unagi Menu

Unagi meat is cooked by skewering fillet strips about five inches long and four inches wide, dipping them repeatedly into a sweet brown sauce, or *tare*, and grilling them over a hot bed on charcoal. But it is not only the meat which is eaten. The backbone of the eel (*ho-ne*), toasted and salted, makes a crispy hors d'ouevre, reminiscent of Triscuit cocktail crackers. The eel liver is invariably used to flavor the small bowl of clear soup (scented with *mitsuba* seasoning) which comes with any meal at an *unagi-ya*. Try the liver; it is most firm and nutritions. At higher class restaurants, the *unagi* head is pickled into a sour *pâté*, or *tsukudani*. At every meal, pickles will be served as a postprandial refresher. And don't forget to sprinkle the tangy Japanese pepper, *sanshonomi* on top of the eel for flavoring.

Kabayaki the grilled (*yaki*) meat, is so called because in former times, the fillet of *unagi* was skewered, length-wise, so that it resembled a bullrush (*kaba*).

Unagi Course Meals

Unagi teishoku うなぎ定食	Includes Japanese salad, *unagi kabayaki*, *miso* soup, rice, pickles
Unaju うな重	Broiled *unagi* on rice in a lacquer box with a sweet sauce. *Unaju*, like *unagi teishoku*, come in several sizes which can be ordered as follows: Regular: *Unaju no nami o kudasai* Choice: *Unaju no jo o kudasai* Special: *Unaju no tokujo o kudasai*
Unazukushi うなづくし	A full-course meal which includes the entire eel, broiled meat, bones, liver soup, etc.

A La Carte Unagi Menu

Kabayaki かば焼き	Broiled and basted eel in two quantities: Regular: *Nami* Top-class: *Jo*
Ikada-yaki いかだ焼き	Small-sized eel is skewered side-by-side in the shape of a raft or *ikada*

Kimo-yaki 肝焼き	Eel livers liberally basted, served with fresh ginger
Kurikara-maki くりから巻き	Eel too small to skewer, called *meso*, are wound onto a spit
Shirayaki 白焼き	Eel broiled until it is "white," that is, *shira*, in Japanese
Umaki う巻き	Eel wrapped in an omelette
Unagi nabe うなぎなべ	Eel and vegetable stew
Unagi-zushi うなぎずし	Broiled eel on a "finger" of rice
Yanagawa nabe 柳川なべ	Baked egg and eel, or more usually loaches (see section below)
Yawata-maki やわた巻き	Eel fillet twirled onto a burdock root, basted and broiled

●

DOJO

The loach, or *dojo*, is a little cousin of the eel, barely six inches long, which has also given rise to its own specialty restaurant. Like *unagi*, backbone hors d'oeuvres and *kabayaki* (eaten with diced eels) are available, but peculiar to loaches is a dish called *yanagawa-nabe* in which loaches are baked with eggs in a sweet sauce in a special earthenware container.

For the adventurous, high-class restaurants such as Komagata, serve a tofu dish called *jigoku-nabe* or "hell pot," made by tossing live loaches into boiling water. The loaches take refuge by wriggling into the tofu, and are cooked alive.

Voilá! an epicure's devilish delight.

▲ Loach omlette (*Yanagawa nabe*)

Recommended Restaurants

Type of Food	Zone	Restaurant Name	Map-Rest. No.	Floor
Dojo	Shibuya	☆ KOMAGATA DOJO	22–1	1F
Unagi	Akasaka	☆ MINOWA	2–4	1F
Unagi	Asakusa	☆ YAKKO	4–9	1F
Unagi	Asakusa	☆ KOYANAGI	5–2	1F
Unagi	Asakusa	☆ TSURU-YA	5–8	1F
Unagi	Asakusa	☆ KAWAMATSU	5–10	1F
Unagi	Ginza	☆ DAISAKU	7–14	1F
Unagi	Ginza	☆ ICHIMATSU	8–21	1F
Unagi	Nihombashi	☆ NODAIWA	17–9	4F
Unagi	Shibuya	☆ IRIFUNE	22–2	1F
Unagi	Shibuya	☆ YAMABUKI	22–24	1F
Unagi	Shibuya	☆ MATSUKAWA	24–10	1F
Unagi	Shibuya	☆ UNATETSU	24–17	1F
Unagi	Shimbashi	☆ OWADA HONTEN	27–17	1F
Unagi	Tsukiji	☆ MIYAGAWA HONTEN	37–6	1F
Unagi	Ueno	☆ IZUEI	39–1	1F
Unagi	Ueno	☆ BENKEI	39–14	1F

● Casserole Kitchens:
Kamameshi

Perplexed by the Japanese penchant for eating gobs of white rice, plain? Then *kamameshi* may be for you, for the rice does not come sticky or naked, but laden with meat, vegetables and mushrooms, as rich as a Spanish *paella* (see color photo on page 162). Each serving of *kamameshi* is prepared and served in its own little cast-iron kettle *(kama)* with a distinctive heavy wooden top which traps and steams the toppings' flavor and fragrance right into the cooked rice *(meshi)*. Trapped also, by this simple, traditional rice-cooker, is the key to the rice mystique.

●

Rice and Kamameshi in Japanese History

That the Japanese word for "rice" and "meal" are identical *(gohan)* is one of the first clues to the emphasis Japanese place on rice. What Westerners might consider the "main dish" of the meal—fish and meat —is simply called *okazu*, or "accompanying dish," by the Japanese. In fact, the equivalent to a lunchbox sandwich is just a triangular ball of rice wrapped in seaweed *nigiri-meshi*, containing a single nugget of salty fish or a sour plum. Even at sumptuous banquets, a bowl of rice porridge (*chazuke* rice "pickled" in hot green tea) caps off the meal, since the food which has preceded it, no matter how voluminous, cannot quite fill the stomach of a person who eats a daily rice diet.

For centuries, peasants and samurai payed their taxes in rice grain and offered it, as Japanese still do today, to the gods. At festivals and on ritual occasions, rice is the ceremonial food: either in the form of *mochi* (a dough kneaded from cooked rice) or *sekihan* (rice cooked with red beans). In its distilled form, as *sake*, rice is Japan's major liquor and cooking wine and fills the chalice which joins man and wife. It is offered to departed souls to eat, in a bowl with chopsticks eerily plunged in upright. It is also the main ingredient of crispy *senbei* crackers, and of Japanese children's favorite dumpling candy, *dango*. Good table manners at dictate that not a grain remain, and that no foreign ingredient defile one's rice bowl—so deep-rooted is the rice culture.

The very process of making rice is as close to ritual as it is to etiquette. About a thousand years ago (in the Heian period), the Japanese started boiling their *meshi* rice in heavy-lipped iron *kama* pots covered with a wooden lid and set into kiln-like stoves. An elaborate procedure, from washing without bruising the grains to constant flame adjustment, produces perfect rice. As if to make the recipe more exacting, other ingredients were then used to embellish the rice, and *voilá*, *kamameshi* (a complete meal) was born.

●
Recognizing a Kamameshi Restaurant

The cast-iron kettle and its curious two-legged top are signs of a *kamameshi* restaurant, usually displayed in front of the restaurant. *Kamameshi* is also often served at *yakitori* restaurants since the *yakitori*, as delicious as it may be, is not a very filling meal unless you eat lots of it.

▲ Japanese casseroles (*Kamameshi*)

●
Gourmet Tips

Once you have tasted rice which has been prepared by an expert, it is easy to understand why this grain has been elevated to the status of a full meal. It is said that in some Japanese haute cuisine restaurants, there is one chef responsible for nothing else but boiling the rice. After all, the reputation of the restaurant in a rice eating culture demands it.

● Ordering from the Kamameshi Menu

A typical kamameshi menu offers the following selections:

A La Carte Kamameshi Menu

Abalone	*Awabi* あわび
Bamboo shoots	*Takenoko* たけのこ
Chestnuts	*Kuri* くり
Chicken	*Tori* 鳥
Crab	*Kani* かに
"Five ingredients" (usually, mushrooms, dried ground slices, carrots, peas and a seasonal vegetable)	*Gomoku* 五目
Oriental black mushroom	*Shiitake* しいたけ
Pine mushroom (Japan's version of truffles)	*Matsutake* まつたけ
Oyster	*Kaki* カキ
Salmon	*Sake* 鮭
Shrimp	*Ebi* えび
Scallop or clam meat	*Kaibashira* 貝柱 *Hamaguri* はまぐり

Other Rice Dishes Available in Japan

Chazuke 茶づけ
Hot tea poured over a bowl of rice sprinkled with slices of salted salmon (*sake*) or a spicy plum, (*umeboshi*), dried *nori* and other seasonings

Domburi どんぶり
A deep bowl of rice topped with tempura, eggs and chicken or pork cutlets (see the chapter on **SOBA**, page 140, for varieties normally available)

Nigiri-meshi にぎりめし
Cooked rice balls (triangular in shape) which are enclosed in a crispy sheet of seaweed (*nori*) and served as a cold lunchbox snack

Yaki-onigiri 焼きおにぎり
Grilled rice balls which are surprisingly delicous and definitely worth trying; usually served at a *Robatayaki* restaurant

Other regional variations of *meshi* dishes are listed in the **KYODO-RYORI** chapter, page 28.

Recommended Restaurants

Type of Food	Zone	Restaurant Name	Map-Rest. No.	Floor
Kamameshi	Asakusa	☆ EDOSADA	4–15	1F
Kamameshi	Asakusa	☆ KAMAMESHI HARU	4–18	1F
Kamameshi	Asakusa	☆ FUTABA	4–25	1F
Kamameshi	Asakusa	☆ ASADORI	5–3	1F
Kamameshi	Ginza	SEIGETSUDO	10–7	B2
Kamameshi	Ginza	YOSSO	15–10	6F
Kamameshi	Shibuya	TEPPO-YA	22–16	7F
Kamameshi	Shinjuku	WAKAMATSU	35–22	7F
Kamameshi	Tsukiji	TORIHARU	37–11	1F
Kamameshi	Ueno	☆ KAMAMESHI HARU	39–7	1F

● Cauldron Cuisines:
Nabemono and Sumo Chanko-Nabe

Nabemono, or literally "things-in-a-pot," is the bouilla-baisse of Japanese food. The ingredients, fresh cut vegetables, mushrooms, *tofu*, firm whitemeat fish, or chicken, are artfully displayed and brought to the diner's table on a platter together with a communal earthenware pot containing a delicious broth (see color photo on page 163). Everything is then set brewing in the middle of the table where the diners themselves, add, tend and select their own favorite tidbits. *Nabemono* demonstrates the elegant simplicity of Japanese cuisine.

●
History of Nabemono

The *nabe*, or "pot" which spawned the one-pot repast, is the traditional cooking utensil of the farmhouse. A thick-walled earthenware casserole, or a heavy cast-iron soup kettle would hang over the open hearth or *irori*. Into it would go everything to keep a family warm and nourished in the midst of Japan's Snow Country.

The dish became popular in old Edo (the name of Tokyo prior to 1868), where newcomers from the provinces sought to preserve a sense of their communal origins.

Recognizing a Nabemono Restaurant

The surest sign that you've come upon a *nabemono* restaurant is to spot a large cauldron hung out front. A few inkbrush strokes might replace this signpost; depicting the wealth of ingredients to be squeezed into the pot. Or, in the wax window-display one might notice an inviting stack of such ingredients, outlarging their *nabe*. The exterior of the restaurant, needless to say, will be rustic, for *nabemono* recreate the no-nonsense farmhouse meal.

Atmosphere and Service

According to the rules of normal Japanese etiquette, it is impolite to use one's chopsticks to pick up food from a communal dish unless, of course, one has turned them around to use the back end. In the case of *nabemono*, however, this caveat is ignored, or should we say, *nabemono* are the exception that prove the rule. "Would you like to share the same pot with me?" is the unspoken invitation to friendship that the dish expresses. No wonder, therefore, that the restaurants are among the most convivial, and the service is the most down-home of Japanese cuisine.

After the waitress has set the pot on the burner, lit the gas for you, and brought out the sumptuous platter of perfectly cut ingredients, she'll hardly pay you a wink of attention, except to adjust the flame and ask "Is everything all right?" A useful phrase to know is:

—Please turn off (down) the gas
火を消して（下げて）ください
Hi o keshite (sagete) kudasai

Gourmet Tips

The gourmet will appreciate the even matching of light-flavored fish to the more subtle vegetables, such as cabbage. Woody mushrooms are used to balance the richer flavors of the fish offerings. Diners can order a second platter containing the partial or full line of ingredients.

Ordering from the Nabemono Menu

Together with a bowl of steaming white rice, and a vinaigrette (*sunomono*) or tiny salad (*aemono*), *nabemono* is a complete bouillabaisse banquet fit for a king. (Indeed, read on about sumo wrestlers' own special *chanko-nabe* version!) The standard dish will include vegetables and fish (or meat), in the ratio of two-to-one. The vegetables include Chinese cabbage, spinach, edible chrysanthemum leaves (*shungiku* or *kikuna*), white delicate *enokidake* mushroom, *shirataki* (chewy filaments made from *konnyaku* devil's tongue root), leeks, parboiled turnips, giant white radish, potatoes and more. On the fish side, cod or sea bream, or with heavy fare, the oilier tuna or yellowtail are used. Chicken, and rarely, beef, is another entre. In ordering, one need only to decipher the list of ingredients, and whether the broth is clear or creamy, the latter being suited for meat dishes.

The Nabemono Menu

Chicken *nabe*	*Tori no mizutaki* 鳥の水炊き
Cod fish *nabe*	*Tara-nabe* たらなべ
Loach *nabe*	*Yanagawa-nabe* 柳川なべ

Oyster *nabe*	*Dote-nabe* 土手なべ
Salmon chunks and potato *nabe*	*Ishikari-nabe* 石狩なべ
Scallop *nabe*	*Hotategai-nabe* ほたて貝なべ
Sea bream or *fugu nabe* with bones and all	*Chiri-nabe* ちりなべ
Sea bream *nabe* without any bones	*Suki-nabe* すきなべ
Soft-shelled turtle *nabe*	*Suppon-nabe* すっぽんなべ
Udon noodles *nabe* with fish	*Udon-suki* うどんすき
Vegetable *nabe* with chicken or fish	*Yose-nabe* 寄せなべ

At the end of the meal, the *nabe* broth is often used by the waitress to make the diner's choice of: *zosui* (rice porridge) or *udon* noodles.

●

SUMO CHANKO-NABE

Chanko-nabe, like other *nabemono*, is a rich stew of vegetables, fish and meat, but its motifs and style come from the *sumo* world. Whereas other *nabemono* emphasize the beauty and bountifulness of the meal by artfully displaying the ingredients, *chanko-nabe* emphasizes the heartiness and king-size associated with the *sumo* wrestler. Here, a large pot is brought to the table, already brim-full of vegetables and meats, and a huge feast is set a boiling in front of the diners (see color photo on page 163). For the hungry diner, a satisfying meal is guaranteed.

History of Chanko-Nabe

The *chanko-nabe* dishes were developed as a training and body-building food for *sumo* wrestlers. The word *chanko* has a very homey sound as it is derived from *chan*, the intimate family form of address since this is how the novices who prepare the food address their elders and idols.

In general, the ingredients of *chanko-nabe* are cheaper than those of *nabemono* because in the *sumo* world, only the highest ranking wrestlers are paid a salary and also, because the visual display of the ingredients at the table is secondary for giant *sumo* wrestlers. They are mainly interested in chowing down. In fact, *sumo* wrestlers sometimes simply boil a pot full of meats chopped across the bone with vegetables shredded in their powerful hands.

Sumo wrestlers live and work together at their coach's gym, or "stable." They eat only twice a day: after their morning practice at 11:00 a.m. and again at 7:00 p.m. It is believed that food "sticks to their bones" better after the sixty-minute period of heavy exercise in the morning.

The well-known American-born *sumo* wrestler, Jesse Kuhaulua—known in *sumo* circles as Takamiyama ("mountain seen on high")—described his first impressions of eating in a *sumo* stable in 1964 as follows:

"The stablemaster and other *oyakata* (bosses) sit down first, then the highest ranked *sekitori* wrestlers, and so on down to the lowliest, who must wait until everyone else has had his fill and picked out all the choicest morsels. We were told that if we wanted to eat well, we'd just have to train hard and become *sekitori* wrestlers."

The reader will not be surprised to know that Takamiyama who is six foot three (191 cm), weighing in at 438 pounds (198.5 kgs) did exactly what his coach suggested and fought his way to the top. Gourmets, be thankful that you get all the good bits without any of the training!

●

Atmosphere and Service

Chanko-nabe restaurants are often decorated with *sumo* pictures and paraphernalia. Any "fat" man behind the counter is sure to lend a jolly atmosphere to a *chanko-nabe* restaurant. This is because the Japanese consider *sumo* wrestlers to be entertainers. They are often excellent singers, as attested to by the many wrestlers' recordings of *enka*—a Japanese ballad form of singing. Long years of apprenticeship prepare the *sumotori*'s skill both as a celebrity and a cook and so it's not surprising that many retired *sumo* wrestlers open restaurants, both the *chanko-nabe* variety and others.

▲ Japanese *Sumo* wrestlers

Ordering from the Chanko-Nabe Menu

There are many varieties of *chanko*—chicken, fish, pork, beef or shrimp. The largest *chanko-nabe* restaurant chain, Edosawa, ranks them in the above symbolic order using the names of *sumo* rankings—*sekiwake chanko*, *ozeki chanko* and *yokozuna chanko*. Above these is a *nabe* type of service—*ozeki yagura* and *yokozuna yagura*. The broth is always a rich and delicious concoction of vinegar, soy sauce, and sugar, while staple ingredients include carrots, cabbage, onions, and bean curd. If you are leary of strong fish smells, stick to the meat and chicken varieties, of which there are plenty.

The Chanko-Nabe Menu

Chicken	*Toriniku chanko* 鳥肉ちゃんこ
Fish	*Sakana chanko* 魚ちゃんこ
Pork	*Butaniku chanko* 豚肉ちゃんこ
Beef	*Gyuniku chanko* 牛肉ちゃんこ
Shrimp	*Ebi chanko* えびちゃんこ

Recommended Restaurants

Type of Food	Zone	Restaurant Name	Map-Rest. No.	Floor
Chanko-nabe	Ginza	YOSHIBA	10–18	1F
Chanko-nabe	Ginza	☆ KASHIWADO	13–22	4F
Chanko-nabe	Ginza	TSUKUMO	14–10	2F
Chanko-nabe	Shibuya	TANIKAZE	24–21	B1
Nabe	Shimbashi	HATSUFUJI	27–11	1F
Nabe/anko	Shibuya	NAGAYAMON	22–5	4F
Sakura-nabe	Shibuya	HACHIGA	26–2	B1

● Dumpling-and-Broth Pubs:
Oden

In the West, we toss tasty morsels into a crockpot or casserole so that the flavors of the ingredients will mix to form their own distinctive brew. In Japan, there is *oden*: a way of simmering *tofu*, fishcakes and potatoes whole in a rich, sweet broth for days on end. The vittles are then plucked out of the shallow pan, intact, delectably juicy, and with textures spanning spongy, tender, and chewy (see color photo on page 164).

●

History of Oden

The predecessor of oden is *miso dengaku*, a skewered piece of *tofu* toasted and then spread with *miso* paste, which got its name from the comic Japanese *Dengaku* play. The ancient farce included an actor dressed as a heron. His brown top, white skirt and stilt-like legs mirror the *miso*, *tofu* and forked skewer, hence the association. Now the list of ingredients has been broadened beyond *tofu* so that simmered, or so-called *nikomi-oden* has become the staple favorite.

●

Recognizing an Oden Restaurant

There are two types of *oden* restaurants: street-vendor wagons and sit-down establishments. As the weather turns cooler, more and more *oden* wagons, or *yatai* appear on the streets downtown. These portable restaurants unfold into a ten-by-ten shelter where four or five diners sit on stools before a steaming counter. The warm atmosphere of a campfire is unforgettable. The *yatai* are the favorite of penny-pinching "salarymen" looking for a good drink and a hot dinner. The adventurous tourist should try ducking into one and, by pointing out items in the pan (also listed in the menu section below), get the master to serve up a few morsels.

Oden restaurants have few tell-tale features because the window displays, if there are any, feature the non-oden items, so predictable to Japanese is the *oden* fare. The solution is to decipher the *hiragana* (see **KANA ALPHABET FINDER** on page 25), ask someone, or just peek inside to see if there's a shallow counter-length pan of simmering *oden* delicacies.

▲ Steeped-in-broth restaurant front (*Oden-ya*)

Atmosphere and Service

Like the picturesque *oden* wagon, the *oden* restaurant is a down-to-earth eatery and a place for convivial drinking. The *oden* counter, in this respect, resembles a sushi bar, in that it is a good medium for interaction with your chef.

Often the sturdy middle-aged waitresses who populate the *oden-ya* kindly take over the task of selecting the food for you.

▲ *Oden* wagon service

Gourmet Tips

Although the Westerner may find just a little of the very hot mustard in the broth very appealing, the Japanese delight more in the buttery seeped-in flavor and the many textural variations of oden.

The *oden* broth varies from slightly salty to very soy saucy. The connoisseur prefers a shop that nurses its broth endlessly, like Otako in the Ginza which on vacations heats it twice daily and, during three months of renovation, had the precious stuff refrigerated by a tuna specialist.

The fish sausages that are the staple item of *oden-ya* range in texture from the porous *hanpen* of ground shark meat, laced with Japanese yam potato *(yama-imo)* and starch for resilience, to *chikuwa* hard, gelatinous slabs of *kamaboko*.

Tofu specimens vary also, some of egg, some freeze-treated and net-like, some sprinkled with sesame seeds and browned. Experiment and enjoy!

The higher class restaurants offer seasonal specialties like bracken *(warabi)*, royal fern *(zenmai)*, and coltsfoot, a form of wild butterbur *(fuki)*.

● Ordering from the Oden Menu

Moriawase or standard combination, is the safest bet for the newcomer. It generally includes a slab of *tofu*, a taro potato, a huge slice of buttery brown radish, cuttlefish and a carefully tied knot of *kombu* seatangle, which is reminiscent of a candied fruit rind. Hot mustard or *karashi*, comes with the dish. If you are going to try the *konnyaku* (so-called devil's tongue root) which foreigners swear they dislike until it is pointed out that it is part of the *sukiyaki* they love, we suggest you dab it with mustard or cover it with *miso* bean paste, since otherwise it is rather bland. Hot *sake*, *atsukan*, is the perfect accompaniment to oden, especially in the winter months. Complete dinners *(teishoku)* include *miso* soup *(akadashi)*, appetizer *(oshinko)* and a salad of cooked vegetables *(ohitashi)*.

If you decide to go *à la carte*, be sure to try *ganmodoki*, a fried *tofu* pouch stuffed with carrots, burdock, gingko nuts, sesame seeds and more. For the triviaphile, *gammodoki* means "imitation goose." In Western Japan, the plump pouches are called *hiryozu* after the Portuguese fried dough fruit pouch, *filho*, or greek *phyllo* leaves. Some restaurants stuff them with mountain vegetables, even ferns at the right time of year.

From the Pan (The Oden Menu)

(Note: asterisks * indicate recommended items)

Bean curd	*Tofu* とうふ
Burdock root wrapped in seaweed	* *Kobumaki gobo* こぶ巻きごぼう
Broiled fish cake tube	*Chikuwa* ちくわ
Cabbage roll	* *Rooru kyabetsu* ロール・キャベツ
Chicken on skewers	* *Tori gushi* 鳥串
Cuttlefish	*Ika maki* いか巻き
Devil's tongue root gelatin (be sure to get miso paste with it)	*Konnyaku* (bite-sized it is called "*hitokuchi konnyaku*") こんにゃく
Dried gourd shavings	*Kampyo* かんぴょう
Fishcake made with yams and rice flour	*Hampen* はんぺん
Ginko nuts	*Ginnan maki* ぎんなん巻き
Hard-boiled chicken eggs	* *Tamago maki* 卵巻き
Japanese radish	*Daikon* 大根

Quail eggs	* *Uzura no tamago maki* うずらの卵巻き
Octopus on skewers	*Iidako gushi* いいだこ串
Sea tangle of kelp tied in a knot	*Kombu* こんぶ
Shrimp	* *Ebi maki* えび巻き
Sweet potato, taro	*Sato-imo* 里いも
Tofu pouch filled with vegetables	* *Gammodoki* (variations are called "*fukuro zume*" or "*gomoku atsuage*") がんもどき
White fishcake made with cornstarch	*Kamaboko* かまぼこ
Yam	*Yama-imo* 山いも

Dumpling-and-
Broth Pubs

Oden

Recommended Restaurants

Type of Food	Zone	Restaurant Name	Map-Rest. No.	Floor
Oden	Akasaka	OTAKO	3–4	1F
Oden	Ginza	☆ IPPEI	9–8	1F
Oden	Ginza	YASUKO	9–15	1F
Oden	Ginza	☆ OTAKO	14–18	1F
Oden	Nihombashi	OTAKO	18–14	1F
Oden	Nihombashi	SHICHIFUKU	19–8	B1
Oden	Roppongi	IPPEI	21–7	B1
Oden	Shibuya	TSUGI	24–22	B1
Oden	Shibuya	WAKASHIRO	26–5	1F
Oden	Ueno	SHINSEI	38–5	1F

● Seafood and Vegetable Restaurants:
Tempura

As with so many Japanese products, what we admire is not a native Japanese invention, but rather an import which Japanese techniques and ingenuity have perfected. *Tempura*, or batter-coated deep-frying of fresh fish and vegetables, was introduced by Portuguese missionaries in the late 16th century. But it is the Japanese who have elevated this type of cooking to the subtle art of locking the natural flavors of fresh ingredients into a lacy golden coating. No wonder the Japanese have written the word for this heavenly dish with the character for "heaven" (天).

●
Tempura in Japanese History

Although the derivation of the word *tempura* is unclear, whether from *tempora* (the day of abstinence of which Portuguese missionaries ate fish) or the artist's pallet of *temperas*, historians agree that the addiction to the food changed the course of Japanese history. The first Lord of all Japan, Shogun Tokugawa Ieyasu, who lent his name to the three centuries called the Tokugawa Period, was fond of sampling new food delicacies. When a cook, coming all the way from Kyoto, arrived in the capital of Edo and claimed to have a new *tempura* concoction, the ailing lord insisted on trying some.

Despite the warnings of his physicians not to aggravate his stomach condition, he overstuffed himself since he found the *tempura* so delicious, and died several days later.

Tempura was originally a delicious between-meal snack. However, in the hands of Japan's master chefs, *tempura* developed into the art of making non-greasy, crisp, deep-fried morsels. The cheap *tempura* snacks and lunches are still available, but only *tempura* boasts the lacy texture and subtle taste which has won the acclaim of gastronomes the world over (see color photo on page 165).

● Recognizing a Tempura Restaurant

To spot a *tempura* restaurant sign, look for the first letter (天), *ten*. It generally appears in a specialty shop's name, as can be seen in the restaurant names *Ten*ichi, *Ten*kuni, and Hage*ten*, etc. Shop fronts are usually constructed of wood in the traditional style with a slatted sliding door and often have a miniature fish pool and garden. The cloth *noren* curtains over the entryway are generally navy blue with white writing.

● Atmosphere and Service

Tempura restaurants range in atmosphere from street-corner stalls to private rooms. The best type, however, is the unvarnished over-the-counter variety where the chef fries up each item and lays it piping hot in front of the customer on a clean sheet of white rice paper. The paper, spread on a small bamboo basket, is not only decorative, but helps to drain excess oil.

The dexterity with which the chef batters up and dunks each morsel into the boiling oil makes for quite a show. At Tsunahachi, for instance, precision allows for even ice cream to be served after being deep-fried as *tempura*. Often at lunchtime, there is quite a waiting line at the better spots. Sputtering oil and raucous shouts of the waitresses orchestrate the service.

▲ *Tempura* counter service

Gourmet Tips

The secret to *tempura*'s crispiness is in its batter coating or more precisely, the lumps, which are apt to form in the tenuous mixture of egg, ice water and flour. Because these ingredients remain unmixed, each morsel dipped to the bottom of the batter is coated in an egg-water-flour sequence. The batter must be made in small batches and not left to stand. If the flour is mixed too thoroughly moreover, the result will be an armor-like pancake casing, rather than the crispy coating the Japanese call a "cloak" or *koromo*. The Japanese claim that they can tell the difference between *tempura* made by a five-year "novice" and a 20-year veteran, so subtle is the chemistry at work in the *tempura* chef's powdery-ringed batter bowl.

The oil and its temperature is the next point. The expert *tempura* chef can test its temperature by feeling the pressure of the oil on a wooden chopstick plunged to the bottom of the boiling vat. If the oil is too hot, the food will not be cooked evenly, while if it is too cool, it will soak into the batter and make the "cloak" greasy. The *tempura* itself ranges from the snowy white Osaka-style *tempura* fried in an oil mixture light on sesame seed oil, to the bright yellow-gold of *kimpura*, fried with batter heavy with eggyolks.

The *tempura* should be dipped in the accompanying four-inch round saucer of tempura dressing *(tentsuyu)* which is a mixture of fish-based soup stock, sweet *sake (mirin)* and soy sauce. Be sure to mix in the grated radish and ginger found in a separate dish, which will give the sauce the proper tang. Instead of *tentsuyu* sauce, some first-class restaurants give their customers freshly ground toasted sea salt, or simply a lemon wedge.

One should note that although covered in batter, each morsel has been carefully sliced and diced to ensure its utmost flavorfulness. Eggplants are often arranged into a fan-shape, since this symbolizes the auspicious sign to the Japanese of "spreading" or "growing".

●
The Standard Fare

Customers often order *à la carte*, item by item, to get what is in season or posted on the wall. Anything from leeks to lotus roots.

Yet the standard order, or *teishoku* at a *tempura* restaurant generally consists of seaweed salad or *sansai* (mountain vegetables) salad appetizer, followed by the *tempura* of prawn, carrot, whole smelt, mushroom, eggplant, sea eel and a fragrant *shiso* leaf battered on one side. These items are fried up at a comfortable pace for eating hot, and served along with a bowl of rice and *miso* soup. Often a dish of raw cuttlefish or tuna, (lightly brazed as *tataki*) is served along with the *tempura*.

Course meals are ranked according to the number of morsels served, usually between five to eleven, and vary in price accordingly. For the sake of maintaining one's appetite, the *tempura* is served from the smallest to largest items.

Tempura meals often end with *kaki-age*, a mixture of shrimp and scallop, or else carrots and burdock root prepared as *tempura*.

Although course meals are usually graded by poetic names, such as the triplet of Pine (*matsu*), Bamboo (*take*) and Plum (*ume*), or the auspicious pair of Crane (*tsuru*) and Turtle (*kame*), the *nami* (regular), *jo* (choice) and *tokujo* (special) rankings of *teishoku* can be understood anywhere.

Ordering from the Tempura Menu

Course and Set Meals
(Includes *miso* soup, rice and pickles)

Nami teishoku 並定食	* Regular course
Jo teishoku 上定食	* Choice course
Tokujo teishoku 特上定食	* Special course
Tendon 天丼	Two prawn *tempura* on top of a deep bowl of rice with a delicious sauce ladled on top
Kaki-age domburi かき揚げ丼	A shrimp-scallop or diced carrot-burdock root *tempura* mixture replaces the prawn of *tendon*
Bento 弁当	A variety of vegetable or shrimp *tempura* served on top of rice in a lacquered box

A La Carte Tempura Menu
(Note: asterisks * indicate recommended items)

FISH

Abalone	*Awabi* あわび
Crab	*Kani* かに
Cuttlefish	*Ika* いか
Flathead	*Megochi* めごち
Goby	*Haze* はぜ
Gunnel	*Gimpo* ぎんぽ

Mantis shrimp	*Shako* しゃこ
Oyster	*Kaki* カキ
* Prawn	*Ebi* えび
Scallop	*Hotategai* ほたて貝
Scallop centers	*Kaibashira* 貝柱
* Sea eel	*Anago* あなご
Shrimp	*Sakuraebi* さくらえび
Smelt (pond)	*Wakasagi* わかさぎ
Smelt (sea)	*Kisu* きす
* Smelt (sweet)	*Ayu* あゆ
Trout	*Yamame* やまめ
Whitefish	*Shirauo* 白魚

VEGETABLES

Asparagus	*Aspara* アスパラ
Carrot	*Ninjin* にんじん
Eggplant	*Nasu* なす
Ginger root	*Shoga* しょうが
Gingko nuts	*Ginnan* ぎんなん
Green pepper (small)	*Shishito* ししとう
Leek	*Negi* ねぎ
* Lemon-mint leaf	*Shiso* しそ
Lotus root (crispy)	*Renkon* れんこん
Mushroom	*Shiitake* しいたけ
Onion	*Tamanegi* 玉ねぎ

* Squash	*Kabocha* かぼちゃ	
* Sweet potato	*Satsumaimo* さつまいも	
Wild butterbur (spring only)	*Fuki* ふき	

Recommended Restaurants

Type of Food	Zone	Restaurant Name	Map-Rest. No.	Floor
Tempura	Akasaka	☆ TENICHI	1–14	1F
Tempura	Akasaka	☆ KAEDE	1–22	1F
Tempura	Asakusa	☆ EDOKKO	4–1	1F
Tempura	Asakusa	☆ NAKASEI	4–2	1F
Tempura	Asakusa	☆ AO-I MARUSHIN	4–28	1F
Tempura	Asakusa	☆ DAIKOKU-YA	5–1	1F
Tempura	Asakusa	☆ SAN-TEI	5–18	1F
Tempura	Ginza	☆ TAISHIN	7–3	1F
Tempura	Ginza	☆ TENMATSU	7–8	4F
Tempura	Ginza	☆ KOCHO	8–3	B1
Tempura	Ginza	☆ TENKUNI	9–13	B2
Tempura	Ginza	☆ TSUNAHACHI	10–10	8F
Tempura	Ginza	☆ TENICHI	12–22	1F
Tempura	Roppongi	☆ TENSHO	20–7	2F
Tempura	Shibuya	☆ INAGIKU	22–11	8F
Tempura	Shibuya	☆ KOYASU	22–19	B1
Tempura	Shibuya	☆ TSUNAHACHI	24–9	6F
Tempura	Shibuya	☆ TENMATSU	24–25	1F
Tempura	Shinjuku	☆ TENICHI	29–14	B1
Tempura	Shinjuku	☆ INAGIKU	29–17	7F
Tempura	Shinjuku	☆ MINAFUJI	30–14	B1
Tempura	Shinjuku	☆ HAGETEN	32–6	3F
Tempura	Shinjuku	☆ FUNABASHI-YA	35–7	1F
Tempura	Shinjuku	☆ TSUNAHACHI	35–11	1F
Tempura	Tsukiji	☆ OKAME	37–2	1F
Tempura	Ueno	☆ TSUNAHACHI	39–9	5F

Seafood and Vegetable Restaurants

Tempura

● Pork Cutlet Shops:
Tonkatsu and Kushi-age

Unlike the European variety of cutlet which is sauteed in a scant amount of butter or oil, the deep-frying of the Japanese breaded coating produces a flakey surface that tastes like pastry and is so light that it looks like crystallized snowflakes. The restaurants serving this type of cuisine are usually called *tonkatsu-ya* since the service of breaded pork cutlet is inexpensive and has become the most widely consumed dish on the menu. The *ton* stands for pork, and *katsu* is short for *katsu-retsu* (cutlet).

▲ Deep-fried pork cutlet (*Tonkatsu*)

Since practically every type of meat and seafood can be deep-fried in this manner, not only can the menus be extensive, but a parallel style of cooking on skewers (*kushi*) has developed (see color photo on page 166). Such restaurants, which are usually a little more expensive, are appropriately called *kushi-a-ge-ya*.

History of Tonkatsu

When the ban on meat was lifted in the first year after the Meiji Restoration of 1867, beef and pork cutlets became instantly popular as spin-offs of the *tempura* style of deep-fried cooking. Yet pork became the dominant meat in the 1900's. Since then, deep-fried chicken and even fish has always been called simply *furai* (fried things) as a matter of differentiation.

Recognizing a Tonkatsu Restaurant

Specialty *tonkatsu* restaurants can be recognized by the pig motif in their sings or windows, or else by locating the character for pig (豚 *ton*) which is invariably a part of a store's name, as for example in the stores *Ton*ki and *Ton*tei. The outside is decorated in a light unvarnished Japanese style, and the cloth *noren* curtains are generally written in black on white.

Atmosphere and Service

Because of their inexpensiveness, *tonkatsu* restaurants appeal to "salarymen" during the day and their families at night. Where *kushi-age*, or vegetables, meat, or seafoods, breaded and deep fried right on skewers (*kushi*) are served as hors d'ouevres, the restaurants are also popular for drinking in the evening.

Pork Cutlet Shops
Tonkatsu
Kushi-Age

Gourmet Tips

Some establishment concoct their own special Worcestershire-like sauce, of roasted sesame seeds (for instance, at Saboten), while those that serve *kushi-age* (restaurants which we highly recommend) often provide a different sauce for each skewer combination, depending on whether it includes vegetables or seafood.

▲ Deep-fried skewers (*Kushi-age*)

Kushi-age, sliced neatly to show the skewered line-up of pork, peppers, onions, eggplant and more, is quite a taste treat, in that the flavors sealed into the bread coating permeate the whole combination. Also worth trying is a croquet (*korokke*) of spiced potato or corn and cream sauce, fried oysters (*kaki furai*) or a hamburger cutlet (*menchi-katsu*).

The Standard Fare

At a *tonkatsu* restaurant, *teishoku* or the set menu, is the most common order. It comes with a pork cutlet sliced into bite-sized pieces on a bed of crisp shaved cabbage, together with a bowl of rice, and one of dark miso soup, and a side dish of pickles. Put some of the sweet and sour Worcestershire *sosu* (sauce) on your meat, or try the special mustard. If you are adverse to fat, try the fillet (*hi-re*) *teishoku* which should be juicy and tender.

●

Ordering from the Tonkatsu Menu

A La Carte Tonkatsu Menu

Assorted tonkatsu	*Tonkatsu teishoku* とんカツ定食
Hamburger, breaded and deep-fried	*Menchi katsu* メンチカツ
Pork fillet	*Hi-re katsu* (or *hi-re katsudon* when it is on a bowl of rice, topped with an egg, peas and onions) ヒレカツ
Pork loin	*Rosu katsu* (or *katsudon* when it is served on top of rice) ロースカツ
Pork slices (fried in ginger without the breaded coating)	*Shoga-yaki* しょうが焼き
Potato croquet (also comes in *koon* creamed corn)	*Korokke* コロッケ
Prawn, breaded and deep-fried	*Ebi-furai* えびフライ

Recommended Restaurants

Type of Food	Zone	Restaurant Name	Map-Rest. No.	Floor
Kushi-age	Ginza	☆ GOMIHATCHIN	14–11	1F
Kushi-age	Shinjuku	☆ TACHIKICHI	35–10	5F
Kushi-katsu	Ginza	☆ KUSHIICHI	12–8	B1
Kushi-katsu	Roppongi	☆ CHISEN	20–4	1F
Kushi-katsu	Roppongi	☆ CHISEN	20–6	1F
Kushi-katsu	Shinjuku	☆ KATSUKUSHI	31–2	B3
Kushi-katsu	Shinjuku	☆ KUSHINOBO	32–7	3F
Tonkatsu	Asakusa	☆ KITAHACHI	4–3	1F
Tonkatsu	Ginza	☆ KAWA	6–17	B1
Tonkatsu	Ginza	☆ TONTSU	13–19	B1
Tonkatsu	Ginza	☆ BAIRIN	13–28	1F
Tonkatsu	Nihombashi	☆ KIGAWA TON-TEI	17–14	B1
Tonkatsu	Nihombashi	☆ SHIN HIRANOYA	19–6	B1
Tonkatsu	Shibuya	☆ KATSUICHI	24–3	1F
Tonkatsu	Shibuya	☆ MIYAMASU-TEI	26–4	1F
Tonkatsu	Shinjuku	☆ TONTON-TEI	35–8	1F
Tonkatsu	Ueno	☆ FUTABA	39–3	1F

● Do-It-Yourself Pizzeria:
Okonomiyaki

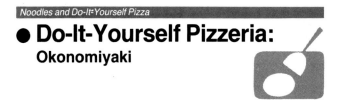

Okonomiyaki, or literally an "as you like it" restaurant, is the Japanese equivalent of a do-it-yourself neighborhood pizzeria, and a most enjoyable form of budget entertainment. Young people typically gather there to make themselves, or at least enjoy watching the chef make, an inexpensive but filling "pizza" which is chock full of meat or vegetables, and topped with Worcestershire sauce, mayonnaise, crisp seaweed, salty fish shavings and more.

●

History of Okonomiyaki

Okonomiyaki originated in Osaka after the war, perhaps as a way of eeking the most out of scarce food resources by stretching them with a lot of pancake dough. Like *takoyaki* (pancake balls with a bit of octopus inside) and *yaki-soba*, or fried noodles, which also rely on Worcestershire-sauce flavoring, *okonomiyaki* is a form of inexpensive food easily cooked on a grill and hence also sold by street vendors.

●

Recognizing Okonomiyaki Restaurants

Okonomiyaki restaurants are located in shopping centers and youth meccas. Look for the cheap plastic block

Do-It-Yourself
Pizzeria
Okonomiyaki

135

letters, often in orange, and the light blue *noren* door curtains which are indicative of this Osaka invention.

● Atmosphere and Service

Okonomiyaki restaurants either have a long narrow counter running along a grill or individual table griddles. Four to six people can generally sit at one table. The atmosphere is plain, cheap prices, and being able to share in making the pancakes with friends, makes

▲ Japanese-style do-it-yourself pizzeria

okonomiyaki restaurants fun and different, and especially popular among young women.

The momentous flip of the giant pancake, and slicing up the pizza-like mass all makes for a convivial ritual.

At counter-style restaurants, you can taste some *okonomiyaki* specialties, like *modan-yaki* (modern *yaki*) which was created just five years ago. The chef will throw two whole eggs with a splat against the grill and then pluck the shells off. He then flips the pancake onto the sunnyside and rotates the whole wad 360 degrees. Watching this avant-garde spectacle can be more fun than making mountains and rivers out of your mashed potatoes.

●

Ordering from the Okonomiyaki Menu

As soon as you're seated at a private grill table, a waitress will come to light the gas jet and paint the table-top grill with oil. Around the walls are signs of *okonomiyaki* ingredients to order. The choice usually includes:

A La Carte Okonomiyaki Menu

Bean curd, grilled	*Tofu-yaki* とうふ焼き
Beef	*Beefu* ビーフ
Clams (short-necked)	*Asari* あさり
Combination: oyster, ham, pork	*Torimaze* とりまぜ
Eggs (see section above for description)	*Modanyaki* モダン焼き
Ham	*Hamu* ハム

Noodles (Chinese style) and cabbage	*Yakisoba* 焼きそば
Omlette	*Omuretsu* オムレツ
Oysters	*Kaki* カキ
Pork	Pooku ボーク
Shrimp	*Ebi* えび
Shrimp and egg	*Ebi-tamago-iri* えび・卵入り
Squid	*Ika* いか

For example, if you choose shrimp, you will get a pre-prepared giant aluminum cup filled with all the necessary ingredients: batter, fresh cabbage, onions, ginger and shrimp, topped off with a raw egg. These things are just laid in the cup and it's up to you to stir them into the batter and then pour the contents onto the hot metal table to cook (see color photo on page 167). The flat spatulas provided are to press the cooking batter flat and to cut the pancake once its done.

The table is furnished with two delicious sauces (or *sosu*): one as thick as honey called *tare* made of Worcestershire sauce and pepper, the other a thinner *shoyu*. Use the brushes to paint them onto the cooking *okonomiyaki* to flavor it and to help hold together the ingredients. Just before it's done, load your "pizza" as thick as you like with fish shaving *(katsuo)* and green seaweed flakes *(aonori)* that will be sitting in condiment bins on the edge of the table. Press these sprinklings into the pancake and flip the whole thing over. One big pancake proves quite a hefty serving.

In summer, the tables are torrid and not even the cold beer can dispel one's running perspiration. On the other hand, in winter, there's not a better, cozier place to go.

Recommended Restaurants

Type of Food	Zone	Restaurant Name	Map-Rest. No.	Floor
Okonomiyaki	Ginza	UTAJA-YA	7–13	1F
Okonomiyaki	Ginza	UNCHOLE	12–3	B2
Okonomiyaki	Ginza	ADORIBU-TEI	13–25	2F
Okonomiyaki	Nihombashi	FUKUJU	19–12	B1
Okonomiyaki	Shimbashi	DAIMONJI	28–3	1F
Okonomiyaki	Shimbashi	FUKUJU	28–6	B1
Okonomiyaki	Shinjuku	TONJU	31–19	B1
Okonomiyaki	Shinjuku	PASU-TAKAN	32–2	3F
Okonomiyaki	Shinjuku	YOCHAN	32–4	4F
Okonomiyaki	Shinjuku	TONKICHI	32–15	B1
Okonomiyaki	Shinjuku	BOTEJU	34–5	6F
Okonomiyaki	Shinjuku	HYAKKA	35–9	1F
Okonomiyaki	Shinjuku	TANUKI	35–12	2F
Okonomiyaki	Shinjuku	TONJU	35–21	B1
Okonomiyaki	Ueno	YANAGAWA KAIKAN	39–22	6F

Do-It-Yourself Pizzeria
Okonomiyaki

● Japanese Noodle Makers:
Soba, Udon and Te-uchi

Lickety-split. That describes Japan's most popular fast food—noodles—served in seconds and devoured with its tasty topping and garnish, all in a zesty broth. The slippery *al dente* strands have a clean, refreshing texture unheard of in the Western noodle!

Some cut-rate *soba* shops around Japan's train stations don't even have seats; customers merely stand at the counter as they eat. A curtain hanging at the entrance to the *soba* stall screens all but their legs and the gusto of their slurps. In the posher spots, however, noodle shops assume the appearance of a Zen retreat in the mountains and serve lumpy hand-beaten *(te-uchi)* buckwheat strands in rough-hewn bamboo frames, or *zaru*.

Soba (buckwheat noodles), and their Osaka cousin, the thick white wheat noodles, *udon*, are a warming meal in winter. In summer, *soba* chilled and dunked in a soy-base sauce laced with shaved yam, seaweed or even *tempura* flakes, is a light, cool snack.

● History of Soba and Noodles

The history of the noodle (both *soba* and *udon*) spans centuries and continents. Brought with Buddhism from China by Japan's first priests in the early ninth century, the noodle is believed also to have found its way in the 12th century to Europe, in Marco Polo's hands. The coarse and unrefined appearance of buckwheat noodles, in particular, appealed to the ascetic tastes of the Buddhists. One Zen sect temple in Asakusa became so rich and famous for its sale of the humble dish to Buddhist pilgrims, that in the 1780's it was forbidden to carry on the pecunious trade. Merchants took over the business and spread the buckwheat blessing among the populace.

The religious origin of *soba* restaurants is borne out by the fact that many of the high-class establishments, such as Rengyoku-an or Mansei-an of Tokyo, carry the suffix *-an* on their names, which means "hermitage." Thus the lowly noodle is purveyed by, on the one hand, the most plebeian, and on the other, by the most sublime *sabi* establishments.

The mental association between long noodles and long-lasting good luck gave rise to the custom of eating New Year's Eve noodles *(toshi koshi soba)*.

●
Recognizing a Soba Restaurant

Although stand-up noodle stalls are easy to spot around stations, the sit-down *soba-ya* is more exclusive. Medium-priced, authentic shops advertise handmade noodles by displaying a man kneading the noodles in the front window (see color photo on page 168). The Japanese-style exterior, with wooden slats on the windows and sliding doors, can be distinguished from other restaurants by singling out the word *soba* (そば) which is invariably written on a white sign in black. Also look for the lunchtime waiting lines or white-jacketed cooks loading the gray earthenware noodle bowls into a silver box balanced on the back of a motorcycle. They deliver *(demae)* the fast food to busy office workers, with the help of the peculiar contraption which fits on the back of their motorcycles and keeps the noodles from sloshing out of the bowl.

▲ Various kinds of Japanese noodles (*Soba*)

●

Atmosphere and Service

No matter how fancy the *soba* restaurant, the noise of Japanese diners slurping their noodles is inescapable because it is considered childish and impolite to cool them by blowing on them. The fancier spots have rustic interiors emphasizing the rough textures of braided straw or bamboo lattice work. In general the more primitive and handcrafted the noodle and decor, the more attentive the service. *Wanko soba*, a dish for which Iwate prefecture is famous, is served by a persistent waitress who sits behind the diner, poised to toss a small lacquer bowlful of noodles into your empty cup of broth. If you are slow to cap your broth, or leave your cup open even a crack, in slosh the *soba* from over your shoulder and you have to finish off another mouthful, ad infinitum.

●
Gourmet Tips

The fact that *udon* and *soba* are more delicious when kneaded by hand (known as *te-uchi*) rather than by machine has given rise to specialty restaurants who employ an expert to handcraft noodles. Besides presenting you with a chance to see how noodles are made—which is fascinating in and of itself—you are guaranteed noodles that are really fresh, and a taste experience unavailable to the spaghetti eater. Many people find the uneven texture of *te-uchi* noodles particularly sensational.

Soba and *udon* do not resemble pasta. Although there are many theories about how to eat spaghetti properly, there is no question in the minds of the Japanese as to how to enjoy *soba*. One must make a great sucking noise, cooling the noodles with the intake of breath, while at the same time swallowing them. Be careful not to choke the first time!

The slithery hard texture of Japanese noodles distinguishes them from absorbent, and pasty pasta. Italians say that pasta must combine with their tomato sauce, in a chemistry appreciated under the tongue, not in the throat. Yet the true *soba* connoisseur eats his cold *soba* plain, after barely flicking the strands into the cup of broth. However, it is acknowledged that the broth is exceedingly delicious, so one Japanese proverb describes the emptiness of the perfectionist as "never being allowed to get enough of the broth." Beware though, since it is considered totally uncivilized to sip or drink the broth plain. Instead, water it down with the hot water used to cook the noodles, which will be served in a large red pitcher.

●

Ordering from the Soba Menu

Soba (buckwheat noodles) are served in two styles: as hot *kake-soba* in a bowl of broth and condiments, or as cold *mori-soba* literally "piled" up on a bamboo lattice in a square frame (*zaru*). *Mori-soba* is dunked in a delicious cold broth, *tsukejiru*, which is served separately. When cold, you should sprinkle the *soba* with

▲ *Soba* noodles come in many different sizes and textures

seaweed shreds. The *tsukejiru* comes with a small dish of grated *wasabi* (horseradish) and finely chopped green onion to be added as a garnish. *Soba* also comes in two colors: brownish gray and green. The green color is due to the addition of powdered green tea, hence the name *cha-soba*.

Udon refers to the thick wheat noodles which are generally served hot in broth, as *kake-udon*. The selection of what you can order to go in the broth (the *kake* part) is similar for both *udon* and *soba*.

Hot Soba and Udon Menu
(especially nice in winter)

Topping	Dish
Bean sprouts	*Moyashi* もやし
Chewy rice cakes	*Mochi* もち
Chicken slices, or sometimes duck	*Kamo Namban* かも南蛮
Chicken and egg (literally, mother and child)	*Oyako Namban* 親子南蛮
Clams (short necked)	*Asari* あさり
Crisped rice cake. Like its nickname "strength," it is invigorating to chew, and a favorite Japanese New Year's food.	*Chikara* 力
Curry sauce is used instead of the bouillon-like fish or soy-flavored broth	*Kare Namban* カレー南蛮

"Five items of food": chicken, mushrooms, *daikon*, etc.	*Gomoku* 五目
Fried bean curd topping named "fox" for the Shinto sprite whose favorite food this is	*Kitsune* きつね
Grated foamy yam	*Tororo* とろろ
"Homely woman" so-called for the woman's face—*okame*—of the *Noh* mask (considered a beauty in ancient times) depicted by the ingredients: fish sausage for her mouth, mushrooms for eyebrows/eyes and a bamboo shoot nose. Also includes wheat cakes and spinach.	*Okame* おかめ
"Moon-viewing". The poetic name refers to "viewing" the egg-yolk topping as the moon through the strands of eggwhite floating on the surface like whispy nighttime clouds	*Tsukimi* 月見
Mountain vegetables such as bamboo roots and bracken	*Sansai* 山菜
Mushrooms. Small, tasty brown mushrooms noted for slithery coating and smooth texture. Served with spinach and grated radish	*Nameko* なめこ
Omelette topping	*Tamago Toji* 卵とじ
Pork slices	*Niku Namban* 肉南蛮

Seaweed	*Wakame* わかめ
Tempura batter flakes are sprinkled on the top, and melt into a jelly-like sauce. Named after the badger or *tanuki*, who is a greasy food freak like his cousin, the fox, according to Japanese legend	*Tanuki* たぬき
Vegetable combo served in a casserole dish with more generous portions of goodies than *okame* ideal for a hearty winter meal	*Nabeyaki* なべ燒き
Vegetables galore!	*Shippoku* しっぽく

Cold Mori and Zaru Soba Menu
(especially nice in summer)

Cold *soba* served on a lacquered tray with shrimp and vegetable *tempura*	*Tenzaru* 天ざる
Grated yam, or *tororo* lopped on top of the noodles	*Yamakake* 山かけ
"Three different colors" of *soba*: green, gray and white	*Sanshoku* 三色

OTHER TYPES OF NOODLES

Hiyamugi 冷やむぎ
In summer, a refreshing thin, white, wheat vermicelli served with a slice of cucumber, tomato, shrimp or even cherries, in a bowl of ice water; the *hiyamugi* is eaten after being dipped in a delectable broth.

Somen そうめん
Thinner hiyamugi

Kishimen きしめん
A flatter, wide *udon* noodle which was invented by a person from Kishu who went to Nagoya during the Edo period. His goal was to make a quicker-boiling version of *udon* to *udon* because of its similarity to flat Italian noodles or linguini. A favorite kishimen dish is *himokawa* which includes spinach, skipjack shavings, fish sausage and some thin fried bean curd strips. Another is *tori kishimen* or chicken in a *kishimen* broth. *Udon* and *kishimen* noodles are also served as the final course in *nabemono* restaurants.

Ramen ラーメン
Chinese egg-noodles

Domburi Rice Dishes
(also available at many noodle shops)

A *domburi* is a large bowl used to serve rice topped with a variety of meat and vegetables. A meal in itself, some common *domburi* dishes are listed below.

Topping	Dish
Beef, sliced paper-thin with onions; the staple offering of the "Beef-in-a-Bowl" fast food chain, Yoshinoya	*Gyudon* 牛丼
Chicken and egg, or literally, "parent and child"	*Oyakodon* 親子丼
Chicken *yakitori* barbecue	*Yakitori domburi* 焼き鳥丼
Fried bean curd	*Kitsune domburi* きつね
Grated yam	*Tororodon* とろろ丼
Mushroom	*Konoha domburi* 木の葉丼
Omelette	*Tamagodon* 卵丼
Pork cutlet	*Katsudon* カツ丼
Shrimp *tempura*	*Tendon* 天丼
Sukiyaki, beef	*Sukiyaki domburi* すき焼き丼
Sweet curry, beef and rice, with a garnish of sweet red pickles, served in a long bowl	*Kare raisu* カレー・ライス
Unagi, eel	*Unadon* うな丼

Recommended Restaurants

Type of Food	Zone	Restaurant Name	Map-Rest. No.	Floor
Kishimen	Ueno	☆ MANSEI-AN	39–19	1F
Soba	Asakusa	☆ CHO-YA	4–27	1F
Soba	Asakusa	☆ OWARI-YA	5–21	1F
Soba	Ginza	☆ YABU SOBA	8–5	B1
Soba	Ginza	☆ MAKI-YA	8–20	2F
Soba	Ginza	☆ CHOJU-AN	13–14	1F
Soba	Roppongi	☆ HONMURA-AN	20–15	2F
Soba	Shinjuku	☆ RANMEN	30–5	B2
Soba	Shinjuku	☆ UMEMOTO	31–13	10F
Soba	Shinjuku	☆ UTA-ANDON	32–9	8F
Soba	Tsukiji	☆ SARASHINA	36–4	1F
Soba	Ueno	☆ YABU SOBA	38–14	1F
Udon	Ginza	☆ FURUICHI-AN	13–4	B1
Udon	Nihombashi	☆ SANUKIJA-YA	16–1	B1
Udon	Shibuya	☆ IZUMO	24–6	5F
Udon	Shibuya	☆ TANIMA	24–18	1F
Te-uchi	Akasaka	☆ ICHIYOSHI	1–2	B1
Te-uchi	Asakusa	CHIKU-AN	5–14	1F
Te-uchi	Ginza	SANUKI TE-UCHI	15–13	1F
Te-uchi	Shibuya	☆ CHOTOKU	26–6	1F
Te-uchi	Shinjuku	USU-YA	30–10	49F
Te-uchi	Shinjuku	SANKI	34–3	8F

● Vegetarian Fare:
Shojin-Ryori

The Buddhist commitment to eating only vegetables has proven to be one of the most beneficial stimulants to perfecting culinary skills in Japan. The reason is simple. To satisfy the palate's desire for a variety of tastes, Buddhist priests introduced an amazing variety of cooking techniques. Their prowess as chefs was so great in fact, that almost all present-day Japanese cooking styles reflect their influence to a large extent. To have a vegetarian meal in Japan is a special gourmet haute cuisine experience.

Although we find vegetarian cuisines delicious, we did not include them in this Guide because vegetarian restaurants (like Sanko-in) and *tofu* restaurants (like Sasa-no-Yuki) are not located in the central districts of the Tokyo metropolis. However, for the adventuresome traveller who wants to seek them out on his own, the main vegetarian cuisines are the following:

Shojin-ryori 精進料理
Zen temple or Buddhist vegetarian cuisine. The word "*shojin*" literally means "to go ahead or progress" (*jin*) "spiritually" (*sho*) and contains the idea that practice is the only real road to doing good. The best restaurants are located near major temples. *Tofu* bean curd is the backbone of this meatless diet.

Sansai-ryori 山菜料理
Mountain vegetable cuisine. Edible wild plants are gathered fresh in all seasons from mountain districts.

Fucha-ryori 普茶料理
Buddhist ceremonial cuisine which developed in Chinese temples. Larger dishes are used to serve four persons at a time and more oil is used in food preparation.

▲ *Shojin-ryori*

Kiritampo Kyodo-Ryori from the Chapter on Regional Specialty Houses (page 28)

▲ *Shabu-shabu* from the Chapter on Beef Fondue Restaurants
(page 56)
◄ *Kaiseki Ryori* from the Chapter on Japanese Haute Cuisine
(page 42)

▲ *Teppanyaki* from the Chapter on Steak Grills (page 59)
▶ *Sukiyaki* from the Chapter on Beef Saute Restaurants
(page 52)

Sushi from the
Chapter on Fresh
Seafood Cuisines (page 64)

Sashimi from the Chapter on
Fresh Seafood Cuisines (page 71)

Robatayaki from the Chapter on Hearthside Grills (page 91)

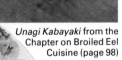

Unagi Kabayaki from the
Chapter on Broiled Eel
Cuisine (page 98)

Fugu-sashi
from the Chapter on
Pufferfish Cuisine (page 80)

161

Kamameshi from the Chapter on Casserole Kitchens (page 104)

Yakitori from the Chapter on Barbecued Chicken Pubs (page 85)

Nabe (above) and
Sumo Wrestler
Chanko-Nabe(left)
from the Chapter on
Cauldron Cuisine
(page 109)

Oden from the Chapter on
Dumpling-and-Broth Pubs
(page 116)

Tempura from the Chapter on Seafood and Vegetable Restaurants (page 122)

▶ *Okonomiyaki* from the Chapter on Do-It-Yourself Pizzeria (page 135)
▼ *Kushi-Age* from the Chapter on Pork Cutlet Shops (page 130)

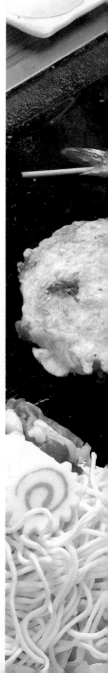

Te-uchi Handmaking of Noodles (above) and the resulting *Udon* (below) from the Chapter on Japanese Noodle Makers (page 140)

HOW TO USE THE MAPS

The next 78 pages of walking maps put at your finger-tips building by building details to ten of Tokyo's major districts so that after you select any restaurant, you can simply walk to it. Other features are listed below.

● Building names on the maps in this Guide are in English. You will find the same words in English on the buildings themselves. The names were selected in this way to be useful in finding your way around a Japanese city like Tokyo.

● The maps clearly indicate subway exit numbers so you can get to your destination quicker using less crowded underground passageways wherever they exist. Letters at each JNR station indicate the colors of train cars: B for blue, G for green, etc.

● All the restaurants are numbered with a two part code on the map: the first part is the Map No. and the second part, the restaurant number. Thus, for example, 3–7 means restaurant No.7 on Map No.3.

● A summary on the right side of each map lists all restaurants on that particular map by number so that you can locate information about the restaurant quick-ly: its name, kind of food served and which building floor it is on.

● Symbols next to the restaurant numbers indicate the main cuisine served at each restaurant. The key to these symbols can be found inside the front cover as part of the RESTAURANT FINDER.

● If you flip through the page tabs on the right side of each map page, you can quickly identify which cuisines are available on that map.

Map No.1 Akasaka

AOYAMA DORI

Roxy •

MISUJI DORI

HITOTSUGI DORI

• 1-1
• Sato

Miami •

AIU •

Belle Vie
Akasaka •

1-5 •

1-6 •

1-7 •

1-8 •

B1

Penthouse •

1-2 ☆ •

1-3 ☆ •

• Shakey's

1-4 • Lopes •

AKASAKA MITSUKE STA
(Ginza Line, Marunouchi Line)

TRACK 1
TO OMOTE SANDO

B2

TRACK 3
TO GINZA

1-17 •

Akasaka
Commerce
Bldg.

Inage-ya •

1-16 ☆ •

1-15 •

1-14 ☆ •

• Mugen

Almond •

• 1-18 ☆

• 1-19

1-12

1-13 •

1-11

1-20 •

1-21 ☆

• Ando

Taj

Kikuya •

Glasgow •

• Akasaka
Floral Plaza

2-1

BAL •

▼Continued on Map No.2

Map No.1 Akasaka

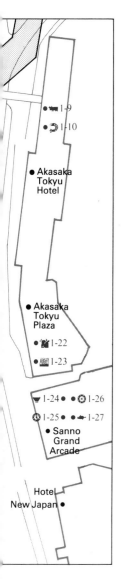

1-1	1F	Matsuba	🍴 Kappo
1-2	B1	☆ Ichiyoshi	🍜 Udon
1-3	B1	☆ Kamado-shogun	🦀 Sakana/kani
1-4	1F	Yushiki	🍤 Sushi
1-5	8F	Horikawa	🐂 Shabu-shabu
1-6	8F	Hoshinoki	◉ Akita
1-7	7F	Ikkyu	🍜 Soba
1-8	8F	Tsunahachi	🍤 Tempura
1-9	1F	Minazuki	🐂 Sukiyaki
1-10	1F	Tenichi	🍤 Tempura
1-11	B1	Mitama	🍢 Kushi-age
1-12	1F	Shogetsu-an	🍜 Soba
1-13	1F	Miyagawa	🍥 Unagi
1-14	1F	☆ Tenichi	🍤 Tempura
1-15	1F	Ebisu	🐡 Fugu/kappo
1-16	1F	☆ Marukin	🐓 Yakitori
1-17	1F	Kushinobo	🍢 Kushi-age
1-18	2F	☆ Kisoji	🐂 Shabu-shabu
1-19	1F	Sharaku	🍤 Sushi
1-20	1F	Chiyono Miyako	🍴 Kappo
1-21	1F	☆ Kaede	🍤 Tempura
1-22	B1	Kangetsu	🍢 Teppanyaki
1-23	B1	Nagaura Soba	🍜 Soba
1-24	1F	Kibun	🍶 Nihon-ryori
1-25	B1	Noto	◉ Nihonkai
1-26	B1	Reisui	◉ Sapporo
1-27	B1	Yachiyo	🍤 Sushi

```
1
2    Akasaka Mitsuke Sta.—Map No. 1
3    Akasaka Sta.—Map No. 3
```

Map No.2 Akasaka

▲Continued on Map No.1

▼Continued on Map No.3

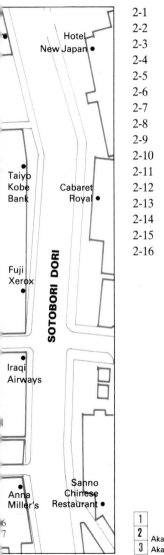

Map No.2 Akasaka

2-1	1F	Hoshin-tei	Soba
2-2	2F	Suehiro	Shabu-shabu
2-3	B1	Reiku	Shabu-shabu
2-4	1F	☆ Minowa	Unagi
2-5	4F	Goraiko	Shabu-shabu
2-6	1F	Noyaki	Robatayaki
2-7	2F	☆ Edogyu	Shabu-shabu
2-8	1F	☆ Neboke	Tosa
2-9	1F	Chacha-tei	Yakitori
2-10	B1	Hamashin	Kappo
2-11	1F	Kushino-ya	Kushi-age
2-12	1F	Koshikawa	Soba
2-13	1F	☆ Okubo	Kappo
2-14	1F	Hozumi	Sushi
2-15	1F	Tsuki-tei	Tempura
2-16	1F	Sushihiro	Sushi

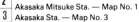

1
2 Akasaka Mitsuke Sta. — Map No. 1
3 Akasaka Sta. — Map No. 3

Map No.3 Akasaka

▲Continued on Map No.2

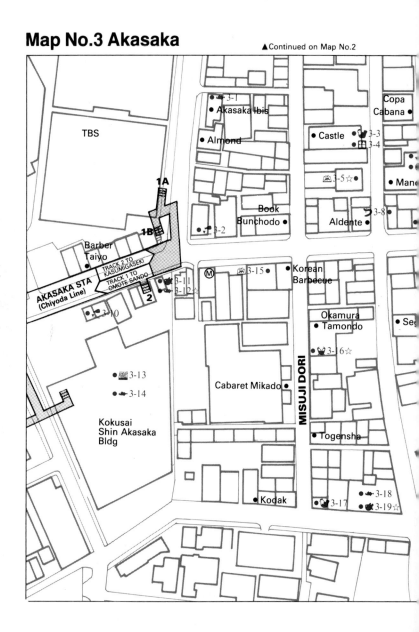

TBS

3-1
Akasaka Ibis
Almond

Castle
3-3
3-4

Copa
Cabana

3-5☆
Man

1A

1B

Book
Bunchodo

Aldente

3-8

3-2

Barber
Taiyo

TRACK 2 TO
KASUMIGASEKI
TRACK 1 TO
OMOTE SANDO

AKASAKA STA
(Chiyoda Line)

3-10

2

3-11
3-12

3-15

Korean
Barbecue

Okamura
Tamondo

Seg

3-16☆

3-13

3-14

Cabaret Mikado

MISUJI DORI

Kokusai
Shin Akasaka
Bldg

Togensha

Kodak

3-17

3-18

3-19☆

Map No.3 Akasaka

3-1	B1	Tsukiji Tamazushi	➤ Sushi
3-2	B1	Ishii	⚮ Kappo
3-3	1F	Tochigi-ya	🐓 Yakitori
3-4	1F	Otako	⊟ Oden
3-5	2F	☆ Inaka-ya	🔥 Robatayaki
3-6	1F	Kappa-tei	⚮ Kappo
3-7	1F	Wan-ya	◉ Akita
3-8	1F	Fukinuki	つ Unagi
3-9	1F	Masuyoshi	➤ Sushi
3-10	5F	Miaji	⚮ Kappo
3-11	2F	Tsukiji	🐡 Fugu
3-12	B1	☆ Kinpa	➤ Sushi
3-13	B1	Sarashina	🍜 Soba
3-14	B1	Fuku-zushi	➤ Sushi
3-15	1F	Ban-ya	🔥 Robatayaki
3-16	1F	☆ Kanidoraku	🦀 Kani
3-17	1F	Torisei	🐓 Yakitori
3-18	1F	Sushikatsu	➤ Sushi
3-19	1F	☆ Takikawa	🐡 Fugu

```
1
2   Akasaka Mitsuke Sta.—Map No. 1
3   Akasaka Sta.—Map No. 3
```

Map No.4 Asakusa

SHIN NAKAMISE DORI

KAMINARIMON DORI

▲ Kappabashi

• Roxy

• Universe

• Saint Louis

(Movie Theater) •

• Viva

• Nagashimaya Cake Shop

4-1

4-2

4-5

4-6

4-7

4-8

4-9

4-10

4-11

4-12

4-13

4-14

4-15

4-16

4-17

4-18

4-19

4-20

4-21

4-22

4-23

4-24

4-25

4-26

4-29

4-30

Map No.4 Asakusa

4-1	1F	☆ Edokko	🍤	Tempura
4-2	1F	☆ Nakasei	🍤	Tempura
4-3	1F	☆ Kitahachi	🐷	Tonkatsu
4-4	2F	Yamakoshi	🐄	Shabu-shabu
4-5	1F	Takara-ya	🍤	Tempura
4-6	1F	Yoneda	🐷	Kushi-age
4-7	1F	Yakko	🥢	Kappo
4-8	1F	Hatsune-zushi	🐟	Sushi
4-9	1F	☆ Yakko	🌀	Unagi
4-10	1F	☆ Sushiyoshi	🐟	Sushi
4-11	1F	☆ Sushihatsu	🐟	Sushi
4-12	1F	Sushisei	🐟	Sushi
4-13	1F	Futaba	🔥	Ikiu-o
4-14	1F	Nagaura	🍜	Soba
4-15	1F	☆ Edosada	🍲	Kamameshi
4-16	1F	Ichimatsu	🐟	Sushi (Osaka)
4-17	1F	Sawashin	🐡	Fugu
4-18	1F	☆ Kamameshi Haru	🍲	Kamameshi
4-19	1F	Daicho	🐟	Sushi
4-20	1F	Genji	🐡	Fugu
4-21	1F	Owari-ya	🍜	Soba
4-22	1F	Tsune-zushi	🐟	Sushi
4-23	1F	Yorimichi	🥢	Kappo
4-24	1F	Yutaka	🐷	Tonkatsu
4-25	1F	☆ Futaba	🍲	Kamameshi
4-26	1F	Mimatsu-zushi	🐟	Sushi
4-27	1F	☆ Cho-ya	🍜	Soba
4-28	1F	☆ Ao-i Marushin	🍤	Tempura
4-29	1F	Okame	🐡	Fugu
4-30	1F	☆ Ichimatsu	🍱	Kaiseki
4-31	1F	Wakashika	🐷	Kushi-age

4 5 Asakusa Sta. — Map No. 5

Map No.5 Asakusa

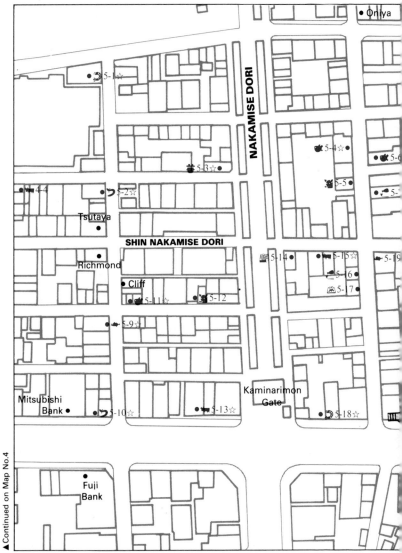

Map No.5 Asakusa

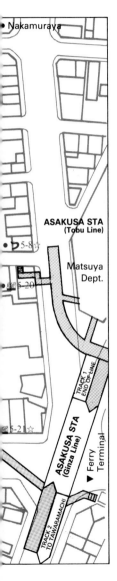

5-1	1F	☆	Daikoku-ya	Tempura
5-2	1F	☆	Koyanagi	Unagi
5-3	1F	☆	Asadori	Kamameshi
5-4	1F	☆	Tsukumo	Fugu/kappo
5-5	1F		Matsumura	Tonkatsu
5-6	1F	☆	Fugukaikan	Fugu/kani
5-7	1F	☆	Tatsumiya	Kappo
5-8	1F	☆	Tsuru-ya	Unagi
5-9	1F	☆	Kibun-zushi	Sushi
5-10	1F	☆	Kawamatsu	Unagi
5-11	1F	☆	Sankaku	Fugu
5-12	1F		Fuji-ya	Tonkatsu
5-13	1F	☆	Chin-ya	Sukiyaki
5-14	1F		Chiku-an	Te-uchi
5-15	1F	☆	Imahan Honten	Sukiyaki
5-16	1F		Hamashin	Kappo
5-17	1F		Sakana-ya	Sakana
5-18	1F	☆	San-tei	Tempura
5-19	1F		Hamashin	Sushi
5-20	1F		Ogawa	Soba
5-21	1F	☆	Owari-ya	Soba

Map No.6 Ginza

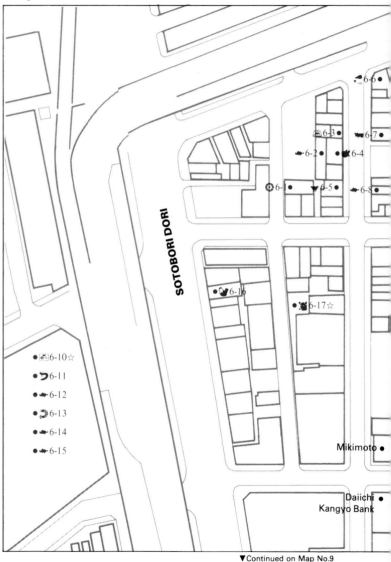

SOTOBORI DORI

6-6
6-3
6-7
6-2
6-4
6-1
6-5
6-8
6-16
6-17☆

6-10☆
6-11
6-12
6-13
6-14
6-15

Mikimoto ●

Daiichi ●
Kangyo Bank

▼Continued on Map No.9

Map No.6 Ginza

6-1	1F	Obako	⊕	Yamagata
6-2	1F	Shincho	🦐	Sushi
6-3	1F	Gyosai	🐟	Sakana
6-4	B1	Tengu	🐡	Fugu
6-5	B1	Waka	🍶	Kisetsu
6-6	1F	Iwato	🍴	Kappo
6-7	1F	Takamatsu	🐖	Shabu-shabu
6-8	1F	Kikaku-zushi	🦐	Sushi
6-9	2F	Ban-ya	🍶	Nihon-ryori
6-10	B1	☆ Awata	🐟	Kyo-ryori
6-11	B1	Benizuru	🔥	Unagi
6-12	B1	Funaki-zushi	🦐	Sushi
6-13	B1	Osome	🍤	Tempura
6-14	B1	Teru-zushi	🦐	Sushi
6-15	1F	Horikawa	🦐	Sushi
6-16	1F	Torikiku	🐓	Yakitori
6-17	B1	☆ Kawa	🐖	Tonkatsu

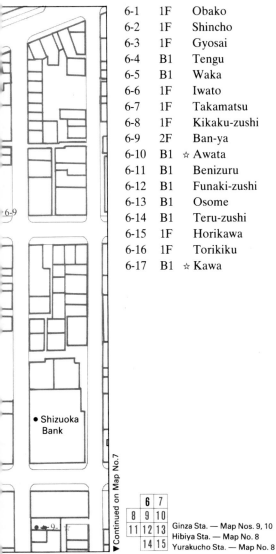

● Shizuoka
Bank

6-9

▼ Continued on Map No.7

	6	7
8	9	10
11	12	13
	14	15

Ginza Sta. — Map Nos. 9, 10
Hibiya Sta. — Map No. 8
Yurakucho Sta. — Map No. 8

Map No.7 Ginza

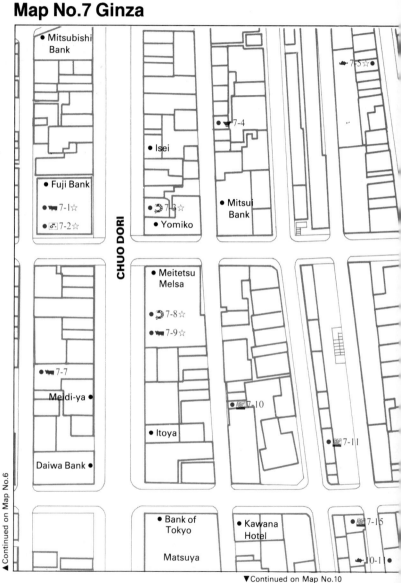

- Mitsubishi Bank
- Fuji Bank
- 7-1 ☆
- 7-2 ☆
- Isei
- 7-4
- 7-5 ☆
- 7-3 ☆
- Yomiko
- Mitsui Bank

CHUO DORI

- Meitetsu Melsa
- 7-8 ☆
- 7-9 ☆
- 7-7
- Meidi-ya
- 7-10
- Itoya
- 7-11
- Daiwa Bank
- Bank of Tokyo
- Kawana Hotel
- 7-15
- Matsuya
- 10-1

▲Continued on Map No.6

▼Continued on Map No.10

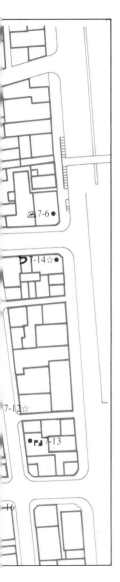

Map No.7 Ginza

7-1	B1	☆ Banban-tei	Shabu-shabu
7-2	B1	☆ Kyotaru	Kaiseki
7-3	1F	☆ Taishin	Tempura
7-4	1F	Koroku	Nihon-ryori
7-5	1F	☆ Yachiyo	Sushi
7-6	1F	Yoshida	Robatayaki
7-7	B1	Takamatsu	Sukiyaki
7-8	4F	☆ Tenmatsu	Tempura
7-9	4F	☆ Kakiyasu	Shabu-shabu
7-10	1F	Ikkyu-an	Soba
7-11	1F	Fukuda	Soba
7-12	1F	☆ Senju	Kappo
7-13	1F	Utaja-ya	Okonomiyaki
7-14	1F	☆ Daisaku	Unagi
7-15	1F	Naokichi	Soba
7-16	1F	Yoshizawa	Sukiyaki

	6	7
8	9	10
11	12	13
	14	15

Ginza Sta.—Map Nos. 9, 10
Hibiya Sta.—Map No. 8
Yurakucho Sta.—Map No. 8

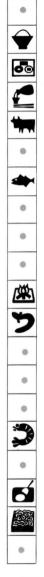

Map No.8 Ginza

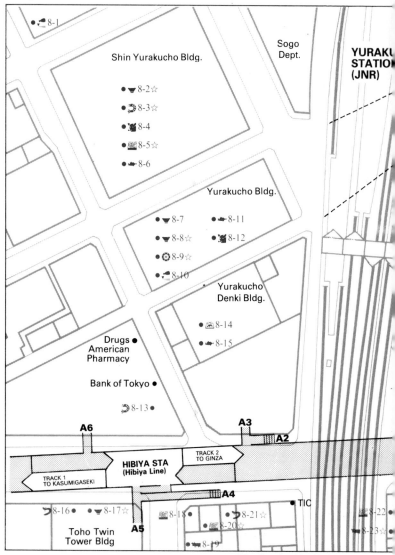

Shin Yurakucho Bldg.

Sogo Dept.

● 8-1

● 8-2☆

● 8-3☆

● 8-4

● 8-5☆

● 8-6

Yurakucho Bldg.

● 8-7 ● 8-11

● 8-8☆ ● 8-12

● 8-9☆

● 8-10

Yurakucho
Denki Bldg.

● 8-14

● 8-15

Drugs ●
American
Pharmacy

Bank of Tokyo ●

8-13 ●

A6

A3

A2

HIBIYA STA
(Hibiya Line)

TRACK 2
TO GINZA

TRACK 1
TO KASUMIGASEKI

A4

TIC

8-16 ● ● 8-17☆

8-18 ●

8-21☆

8-22

A5

● 8-20☆

8-23☆

Toho Twin
Tower Bldg

● 8-19

184

▼Continued on Map No.11

Map No.8 Ginza

8-1	B1	Miyokawa	⌣ Kappo
8-2	B1	☆ Imahan	▼ Nihon-ryori
8-3	B1	☆ Kocho	⤴ Tempura
8-4	B1	Marushige	▉ Tonkatsu
8-5	B1	☆ Yabu Soba	▧ Soba
8-6	B1	Yoshikin	⬌ Sushi
8-7	B1	Tsukushi	▼ Kisetsu
8-8	B1	☆ Izumi	▼ Kisetsu
8-9	B1	☆ Sapporo	◉ Hokkaido
8-10	B1	Tachibana	⌣ Kappo
8-11	B1	Yukishima	⬌ Sushi
8-12	B1	Uraku	▉ Tonkatsu
8-13	B1	Kiyose	⤴ Tempura
8-14	B1	Donto	⛰ Robatayaki
8-15	B1	Sushita	⬌ Sushi
8-16	9F	Owada	つ Unagi
8-17	9F	☆ Shiru Nao	▼ Nihon-ryori
8-18	1F	Dondo	▧ Soba
8-19	4F	Gassan	▨ Shabu-shabu
8-20	2F	☆ Maki-ya	▧ Soba
8-21	1F	☆ Ichimatsu	つ Unagi
8-22	2F	Sarashina	▧ Soba
8-23	1F	☆ Kokonoe	▨ Sukiyaki
8-24	8F	☆ Takao	▨ Shabu-shabu

▼ Continued on Map No.9

New Toho ●
Cinema 1
Cinema 2
8-24 ☆●

	6	7
8	9	10
11	12	13
	14	15

Ginza Sta.—Map Nos. 9, 10
Hibiya Sta.—Map No. 8
Yurakucho Sta.—Map No. 8

Map No.9 Ginza

▲Continued on Map No.6

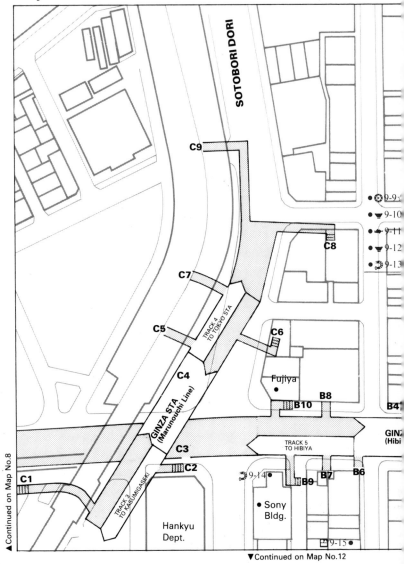

SOTOBORI DORI

C9

C8

● ⊙ 9-9
● ▼ 9-10
● ← 9-11
● ▼ 9-12
● 🚌 9-13

C7

TRACK 4
TO TOKYO STA

C5

C6

C4

Fujiya
●

B8

GINZA STA
(Marunouchi Line)

B10

B4

TRACK 5
TO HIBIYA

GINZA
(Hibi

C3

C2

● 9-14

B6

B9 B7

C1

● Sony
Bldg.

TRACK 3
TO KASUMIGASEKI

Hankyu
Dept.

🏢 9-15 ●

▲Continued on Map No.8

▼Continued on Map No.12

Map No.9 Ginza

9-1	1F	☆ Hatsune-zushi	Sushi
9-2	1F	Hageten	Tempura
9-3	B1	Hagakure	Saga
9-4	3F	Biidoro-tei	Teppanyaki
9-5	4F	Den	Nihon-ryori
9-6	2F	Gyosai	Sushi
9-7	B1	Fuji-ya	Shabu-shabu
9-8	1F	☆ Ippei	Oden
9-9	5F	☆ Akita-ya	Akita
9-10	4F	☆ Asuka	Nihon-ryori
9-11	1F	Kamehachi-zushi	Sushi
9-12	5F	☆ Kinsen	Nihon-ryori
9-13	B2	☆ Tenkuni	Tempura
9-14	B1	Tenichi	Tempura
9-15	1F	Yasuko	Oden

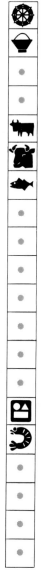

▼Continued on Map No.10

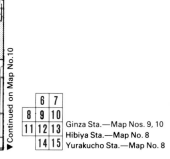

Ginza Sta.—Map Nos. 9, 10
Hibiya Sta.—Map No. 8
Yurakucho Sta.—Map No. 8

Map No.10 Ginza

▲Continued on Map No.7

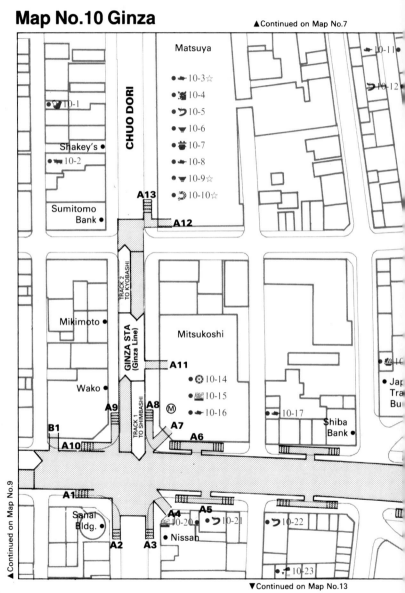

Matsuya

- 🛍 10-3☆
- 🍱 10-4
- 🍜 10-5
- 🍷 10-6
- 🍲 10-7
- 🛍 10-8
- 🍷 10-9☆
- 🍲 10-10☆

CHUO DORI

10-1

Shakey's ●

10-2

Sumitomo Bank ●

A13

A12

TRACK 2 TO KYOBASHI

GINZA STA (Ginza Line)

Mikimoto ●

Mitsukoshi

Wako ●

A11

- ⊙ 10-14
- 🖼 10-15
- 🛍 10-16

A9

A8

Ⓜ

TRACK 1 TO SHIMBASHI

A7

B1

A6

A10

Shiba Bank ●

10-17

Japan Travel Bu

10-11

10-12

10

A1

Sanai Bldg.

A4

A5

10-20

10-21

10-22

● Nissan

A2

A3

10-23

◄Continued on Map No.9

▼Continued on Map No.13

Map No.10 Ginza

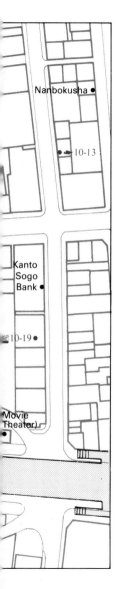

Nanbokusha ●

10-13

Kanto
Sogo
Bank ●

10-19 ●

Movie
Theater)
●

10-1	1F	Atari-ya	Yakitori
10-2	1F	Rangetsu	Sukiyaki
10-3	8F	☆ Fukusuke	Sushi
10-4	B2	Katsushin	Tonkatsu
10-5	8F	Miyagawa	Unagi
10-6	8F	Sagano	Kansai-ryori
10-7	B2	Seigetsudo	Kamameshi
10-8	B2	Sushiden	Sushi
10-9	8F	☆ Tsukiji Tamura	Nihon-ryori
10-10	8F	☆ Tsunahachi	Tempura
10-11	1F	Kotsurugi	Sushi
10-12	1F	Unatetsu	Unagi
10-13	1F	Kiraku-zushi	Sushi
10-14	B3	Jinbei	Inaka
10-15	B3	Sanukija-ya	Udon
10-16	B3	Shusse-zushi	Sushi
10-17	1F	Ginza Hokake-zushi	Sushi
10-18	1F	Yoshiba	Chanko-nabe
10-19	B1	Sanukija-ya	Udon
10-20	1F	Ginza-sarashina	Soba
10-21	1F	Chikuyo-tei	Unagi
10-22	B1	Morishita	Unagi
10-23	1F	Shiki	Kappo

6	7
8	9	10
11	12	13
14	15

Ginza Sta.—Map Nos. 9, 10
Hibiya Sta.—Map No. 8
Yurakucho Sta.—Map No. 8

Map No.11 Ginza

▲Continued on Map No.8

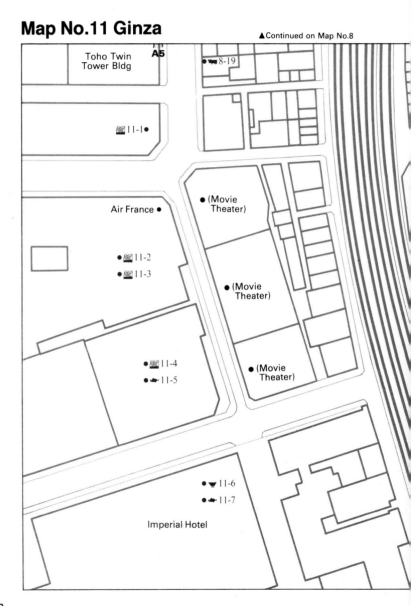

Toho Twin
Tower Bldg

A5

8-19

11-1

(Movie
Theater)

Air France ●

11-2

11-3

(Movie
Theater)

11-4

11-5

(Movie
Theater)

11-6

11-7

Imperial Hotel

Map No.11 Ginza

11-1	B1	Senba Soba	Soba
11-2	B1	Mimikyu	Soba
11-3	B1	Ran-tei	Soba
11-4	B1	Shinanoji	Soba
11-5	B1	Takara	Sushi
11-6	B1	Nadaman	Nihon-ryori
11-7	B1	Nakata	Sushi
11-8	1F	Taiga	Fugu

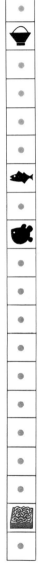

▼ Continued on Map No.12

6	7	
8	9	10
11	12	13
	14	15

Ginza Sta.—Map Nos. 9, 10
Hibiya Sta.—Map No. 8
Yurakucho Sta.—Map No. 8

Map No.12 Ginza

▲Continued on Map No.9

Hankyu Dept.

● ⊃ 12-1
● ⊷ 12-2
● ⌂ 12-3
● 🖼 12-4

Mitsui Bank ●

⏛ 12-5 ☆ ●

● 🍴 12-8 ☆

● ⊷ 12-6

9-15 ●

⊃ 12-7 ●

MIYUKI DORI

● ⊏ 12-19

Josephine ●

⊋ 12-22 ☆ ●

● ⏛ 12-21

Asahi Bldg. ●

● ⊡ 12-20 ☆

SOTOBORI DORI

● ✋ 12-16

● ⊏ 12-17

🍴 12-13 ●
⊷ 12-14 ●

◎ 12-18 ●

⊷ 12-15 ●

◀Continued on Map No.11

● ⏛ 12-24 ☆

● ⊡ 12-25 ☆

● Dentsu

● Daiichi Kangyo Bank

● 🍴 12-26

● Shiseido

⏛

▼Continued on Map No.14

Map No.12 Ginza

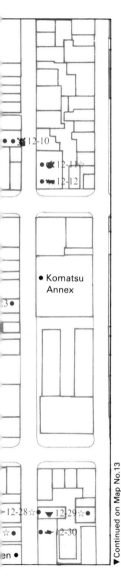

12-1	B2	Iwada	⊃	Unagi
12-2	B1	Tanuki	↤	Sushi
12-3	B2	Unchole	⊟	Okonomiyaki
12-4	B2	Zenkoji Soba	▦	Soba
12-5	1F	☆ Tsubohan	▼	Nihon-ryori
12-6	1F	Uo-ji	↤	Sushi
12-7	1F	Owada	⊃	Unagi
12-8	B1	☆ Kushiichi	▒	Kushi-age
12-9	5F	Toto-ya	⛰	Robatayaki
12-10	3F	Kushinobo	▒	Kushi-katsu
12-11	B1	☆ Tsukiji	⬤	Fugu/kisetsu
12-12	5F	Suehiro	⋈	Shabu-shabu
12-13	1F	Benihana	▓	Teppanyaki
12-14	1F	Sushiko	↤	Sushi
12-15	B1	Sharaku	↤	Sushi
12-16	1F	Kushi Koruza	⬤	Kushi-yaki
12-17	1F	Muto	⋰	Kappo
12-18	4F	Shimazu-tei	⊙	Satsuma
12-19	B1	Yaozen	⋰	Kappo
12-20	B1	☆ Matsuhana	▣	Kaiseki
12-21	1F	Shintaro	▼	Nihon-ryori
12-22	1F	☆ Tenichi	⋑	Tempura
12-23	1F	Kushinobo	▒	Kushi-katsu
12-24	B1	☆ Chinzanso	▼	Kansai-kappo
12-25	B1	☆ Tsujitome	▣	Kaiseki
12-26	2F	Toyoda	▒	Tonkatsu
12-27	B1	☆ Gennai	▼	Kansai-kappo
12-28	1F	☆ Kampachi	↤	Sushi
12-29	1F	☆ Hamasaku Honten	▼	Kansai-kappo
12-30	1F	Sharaku	↤	Sushi

6	7
8	9	10
11	**12**	13
14	15

Ginza Sta.—Map Nos. 9, 10
Hibiya Sta.—Map No. 8
Yurakucho Sta.—Map No. 8

▼ Continued on Map No.13

Map No.13 Ginza

▲Continued on Map No.10

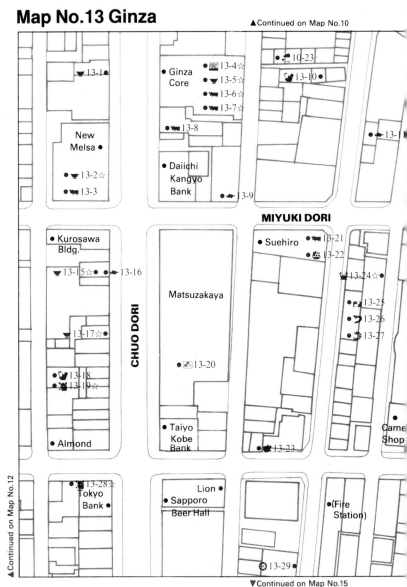

◄Continued on Map No.12

▼Continued on Map No.15

194

Map No.13 Ginza

13-1	7F	Iraka	♥ Kansai-ryori
13-2	8F	☆ Oshima	♥ Nihon-ryori
13-3	8F	Suehiro	🐂 Sukiyaki
13-4	B1	☆ Furuichi-an	🍜 Udon
13-5	B2	☆ Kacho	♥ Nihon-ryori
13-6	B2	☆ Shabusen	🐂 Shabu-shabu
13-7	2F	☆ Shabusen	🐂 Shabu-shabu
13-8	5F	Kisoji	🐂 Shabu-shabu
13-9	3F	Sushikin	🐟 Sushi
13-10	1F	Torifuji	🐔 Yakitori
13-11	1F	☆ Ao-yagi	🐟 Sushi
13-12	B1	☆ Ogura	♥ Kansai-kappo
13-13	1F	☆ Mikasakaikan	🐂 Shabu-shabu
13-14	1F	☆ Choju-an	🍜 Soba
13-15	7F	☆ Tsukiji Uemura	♥ Nihon-ryori
13-16	4F	Tsukiji Tama-zushi	🐟 Sushi
13-17	1F	☆ Ohmasu	♥ Nihon-ryori
13-18	1F	Torishige	🐔 Yakitori
13-19	B1	☆ Tontsu	🐷 Tonkatsu
13-20	7F	Tanguma	🍱 Kyo-ryori
13-21	1F	Suehiro	🐂 Sukiyaki
13-22	4F	Kashiwado	🍲 Chanko-nabe
13-23	1F	Mihara	🐡 Fugu
13-24	1F	☆ Kanisen	🦀 Kani
13-25	2F	Adoribu-tei	Okonomiyaki
13-26	1F	Hyotan-ya	🐍 Unagi
13-27	1F	Tachibana	🦐 Tempura
13-28	1F	☆ Bairin	🐷 Tonkatsu
13-29	B1	Koshikijima	⊕ Kyushu
13-30	1F	Hatsuhana	♥ Nihon-ryori

6	7	
8	9	10
11	12	13
14	15	

Ginza Sta.—Map Nos. 9, 10
Hibiya Sta.—Map No. 8
Yurakucho Sta.—Map No. 8

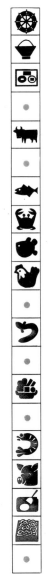

Map No.14 Ginza

▲Continued on Map No.12

● Shiseido

● 14-1☆

14-2 ●

14-3 ●

Coffee Shop
Ranzu ●

14-5☆●

14-4 ●

14-7

Yanase ●

SOTOBORI DORI

● 14-14

14-17

14-11☆

14-12☆●

● 14-13

Art
Coffee ●

Nikko
Hotel ●

14-18☆

14-15 ●

Mitsu
Urbar
Hote
●

● 14-16☆

196

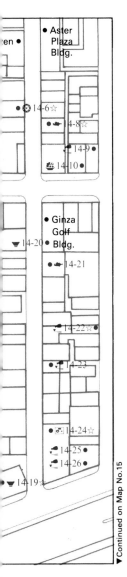

Map No.14 Ginza

14-1	2F	☆ Benkei	🍴 Teppanyaki
14-2	1F	Takefuku	🐡 Fugu
14-3	1F	Gin-zushi	🍣 Sushi
14-4	1F	Sushiko	🍣 Sushi
14-5	7F	☆ Okahan	🍲 Sukiyaki
14-6	1F	☆ Neboke	◎ Tosa
14-7	1F	Manmaru-zushi	🍣 Sushi
14-8	1F	☆ Sushiko	🍣 Sushi
14-9	B1	Amano	🍵 Kappo
14-10	2F	Tsukumo	🍲 Chanko-nabe
14-11	1F	☆ Gomihatchin	🍢 Kushi-age
14-12	B1	☆ Hiiragi	🍲 Shabu-shabu
14-13	1F	Ozawa	🍣 Sushi
14-14	1F	Yamazaki	🍵 Kansai-kappo
14-15	6F	Mihara	🍤 Tempura
14-16	1F	☆ Uo-masa	🍣 Sushi
14-17	B1	Sushigin	🍣 Sushi
14-18	1F	☆ Otako	🍱 Oden
14-19	B1	☆ Munakata	🍵 Nihon-ryori
14-20	7F	Irori	🍵 Nihon-ryori
14-21	1F	Kampachi	🍣 Sushi
14-22	1F	☆ Ohkuma	🍵 Kappo
14-23	1F	Tsukasa	🍵 Kappo
14-24	2F	☆ Unkai	🍱 Kaiseki
14-25	2F	Maeda	🍵 Kappo
14-26	5F	Tomikawa	🍵 Kappo

▶ Continued on Map No.15

Ginza Sta.—Map Nos. 9, 10
Hibiya Sta.—Map No. 8
Yurakucho Sta.—Map No. 8

	6	7	
8	9	10	
11	12	13	
	14	15	

Map No.15 Ginza

▲Continued on Map No.13

▲Continued on Map No.14

15-1☆

Yamato
Bldg.

13-29

Hakata

15-2

15-3

The Ginza

Shiseido
Bldg.

Cafe
Endless

Mitsubishi
Bank

15-23☆

CHUO DORI

15-4☆

15-5

15-6☆

15-10

15-7☆

15-11

15-8

15-12

15-9☆

15-13

15-14☆

15-16☆

15-15

15-17

15-22

15-18

15-20

15-19☆

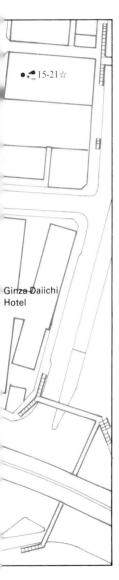

Map No.15 Ginza

15-1	2F	☆ Ginichi	🐡 Fugu
15-2	1F	Shogetsu	🐡 Fugu
15-3	B1	Kiku-zushi	🍤 Sushi
15-4	1F	☆ Hamamura	🍲 Kansai-kappo
15-5	1F	Santomo	🍲 Nihon-ryori
15-6	1F	☆ Umemoto	🍴 Kappo
15-7	1F	☆ Jiro	🍴 Kappo
15-8	2F	Goro	🍲 Nihon-ryori
15-9	5F	☆ Sushikiyo	🍤 Sushi
15-10	6F	Yosso	🍚 Kamameshi
15-11	B1	Hongin	🍤 Sushi
15-12	1F	Tenkuni	🍤 Tempura
15-13	1F	Sanuki Te-uchi	🍜 Te-uchi
15-14	1F	☆ Naruto	🐡 Fugu
15-15	1F	Azuma	🍲 Kisetsu
15-16	1F	☆ Toriman	🐔 Yakitori
15-17	1F	Suehiro	🥩 Shabu-shabu
15-18	B1	Mizuki	🍴 Kappo
15-19	1F	☆ Mikazuki-tei	🐟 Ikizukuri
15-20	3F	Mizutani	🍲 Nihon-ryori
15-21	B1	☆ Seki-tei	🍴 Kappo
15-22	1F	Segawa	🍴 Kappo
15-23	1F	☆ Waraku	🥩 Sukiyaki

6	7	
8	9	10
11	12	13
	14	15

Ginza Sta.—Map Nos. 9, 10
Hibiya Sta.—Map No. 8
Yurakucho Sta.—Map No. 8

Map No.16 Nihombashi

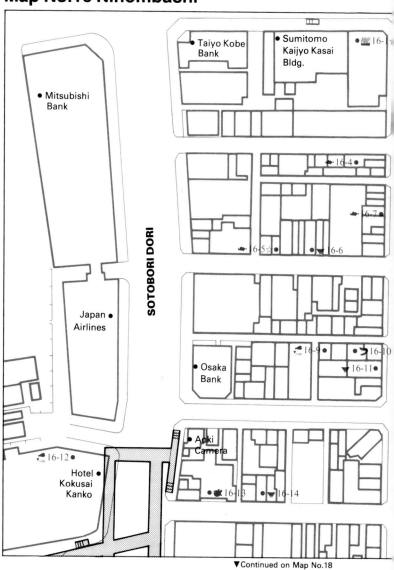

● Mitsubishi
  Bank

● Taiyo Kobe
  Bank

● Sumitomo
  Kaijyo Kasai
  Bldg.

●▒16-

16-4 ●

16-7

16-5☆●   ●▼16-6

SOTOBORI DORI

Japan ●
Airlines

16-9 ●   ● ●16-10
                ▼16-11●

● Osaka
  Bank

● Aoki
  Camera

●16-12 ●

Hotel ●
Kokusai
Kanko

● 16-13   ● ▼16-14

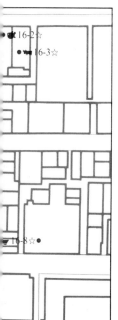

Map No.16 Nihombashi

16-1	B1	☆ Sanukija-ya	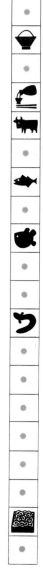 Udon
16-2	B1	☆ Hankyo	Fugu/nabe
16-3	1F	☆ Ao-i	Sukiyaki
16-4	1F	Masu-zushi	Sushi
16-5	1F	☆ Eiraku-zushi	Sushi
16-6	1F	Ranzan	Kisetsu
16-7	1F	Maguro-zushi	Sushi
16-8	B1	☆ Kamogawa	Nihon-ryori
16-9	1F	Takase	Kappo
16-10	1F	Hashimoto	Unagi
16-11	B1	Teru	Wafu/steak
16-12	B1	Tamanohikari	Kappo
16-13	B1	Kapuri	Fugu
16-14	1F	Toyoda	Nihon-ryori
16-15	B1	☆ Munakata	Nihon-ryori

▼ Continued on Map No.17

16	17
18	
19	

Nihombashi Sta. — Map No. 17
Tokyo Sta. — Map No. 18

Map No.17 Nihombashi

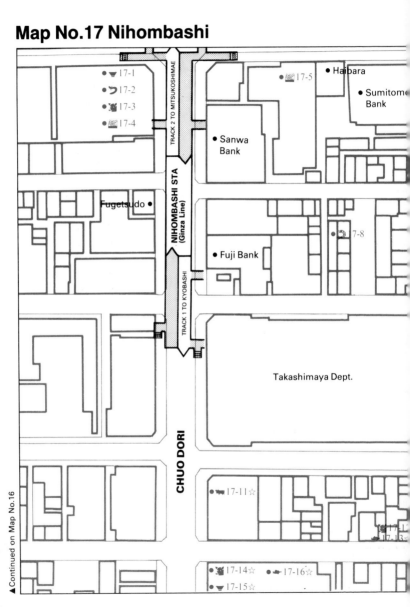

- ▼ 17-1
- つ 17-2
- 🎴 17-3
- 🏯 17-4

TRACK 2 TO MITSUKOSHIMAE

NIHOMBASHI STA (Ginza Line)

TRACK 1 TO KYOBASHI

Fugetsudo ●

- 🏯 17-5
- Haibara
- Sumitomo Bank
- Sanwa Bank
- 🏯 17-8
- Fuji Bank

CHUO DORI

Takashimaya Dept.

- 🍜 17-11 ☆
- 17-12
- 17-13
- 🎴 17-14 ☆
- 17-16 ☆
- ▼ 17-15 ☆

▲ Continued on Map No.16

Map No.17 Nihombashi

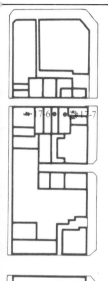

17-1	B2	Ginya	▼ Nihon-ryori
17-2	B2	Maruzen	⊃ Unagi
17-3	B1	Taikou	✖ Tonkatsu
17-4	B2	Yabukyu	▨ Soba
17-5	B1	Asama	▨ Soba
17-6	1F	Matsumi-zushi	➥ Sushi
17-7	1F	Hayashi	⊃ Tempura
17-8	1F	Yatsuhana	⊃ Tempura
17-9	4F	☆ Nodaiwa	⊃ Unagi
17-10	4F	☆ Sangen	▼ Kansai-kappo
17-11	B1	☆ Zakuro	➤ Sukiyaki
17-12	1F	Yajikita	✖ Tonkatsu
17-13	1F	☆ Yoshino-zushi	➥ Sushi
17-14	B1	☆ Kigawa Ton-tei	✖ Tonkatsu
17-15	B1	☆ Uzura	▼ Nihon-ryori
17-16	B1	☆ Yoshino	➥ Sushi

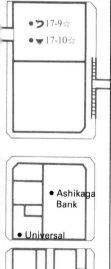

16	17

18	
19	Nihombashi Sta. — Map No. 17
	Tokyo Sta. — Map No. 18

Map No.18 Nihombashi

▲Continued on Map No.16

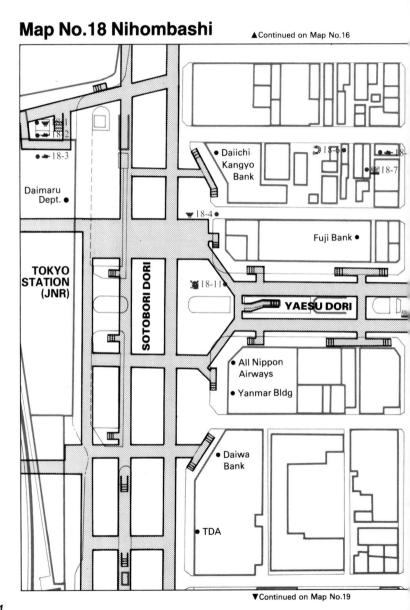

18-1

18-2

18-3

18-6 18-

18-7

Daiichi Kangyo Bank

Daimaru Dept. ●

18-4 ●

Fuji Bank ●

TOKYO STATION (JNR)

SOTOBORI DORI

18-11

YAESU DORI

● All Nippon Airways

● Yanmar Bldg

● Daiwa Bank

● TDA

▼Continued on Map No.19

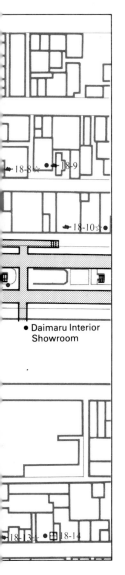

Map No.18 Nihombashi

18-1	B1	Kitahama	▼ Kansai-kappo
18-2	B1	Sinoda-zushi	➤ Sushi
18-3	B1	Futaba-zushi	➤ Sushi
18-4	B1	Hatsufuji	▼ Nihon-ryori
18-5	1F	Masu-zushi	➤ Sushi
18-6	1F	Tenhachi	➣ Tempura
18-7	1F	Yanagi	▦ Soba
18-8	2F	☆ Sushitetsu	➤ Sushi
18-9	1F	Horai	➤ Sushi
18-10	B1	☆ Sushi-kyu	➤ Sushi
18-11	B1	Shin Hirano-ya	🐷 Tonkatsu
18-12	B1	Joban-tei	▦ Soba
18-13	1F	☆ Hatsune-zushi	➤ Sushi
18-14	1F	Otako	▣ Oden

• Daimaru Interior
Showroom

16	17
18	

Nihombashi Sta. — Map No. 17

| 19 | Tokyo Sta. — Map No. 18 |

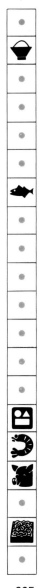

Map No.19 Nihombashi

▲Continued on Map No.18

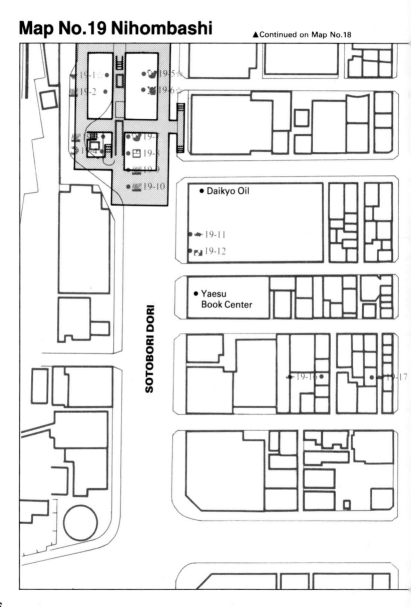

19-1

19-2

19-5☆

19-6☆

19-

19-

19-10

● Daikyo Oil

19-11

19-12

● Yaesu
Book Center

19-16

19-17

SOTOBORI DORI

Map No.19 Nihombashi

19-1	B1	☆ Otakubo	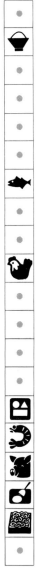 Kisetsu
19-2	B1	Hakata Udon	Udon
19-3	B1	Hyakumangoku	Udon
19-4	B1	Kanesei	Tempura
19-5	B1	☆ Tohachi	Yakitori
19-6	B1	☆ Shin Hiranoya	Tonkatsu
19-7	B1	Zen-ya	Yakitori
19-8	B1	Shichifuku	Oden
19-9	B1	Otafuku	Soba
19-10	B1	Bonchi	Soba
19-11	B1	Sinoda-zushi	Sushi
19-12	B1	Fukuju	Okonomiyaki
19-13	1F	Nihachi Soba	Soba
19-14	1F	Kyo-zushi	Sushi
19-15	1F	Yamamuto	Soba
19-16	1F	Edohachi-zushi	Sushi
19-17	1F	Kiku-zushi	Sushi

16 17
18
19 Nihombashi Sta. — Map No. 17
Tokyo Sta. — Map No. 18

Map No.20 Roppongi

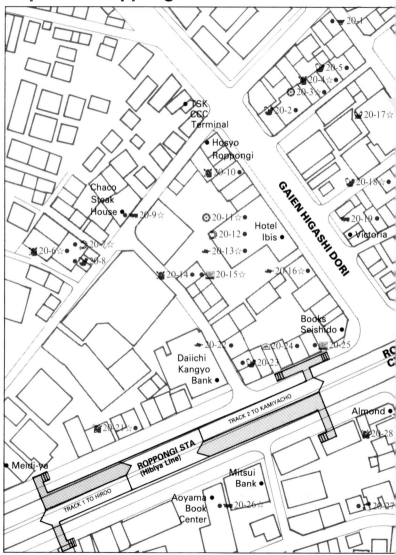

● 20-1

● 20-5 ●
● 20-4 ☆
◉ 20-3 ☆
● 20-2 ●
📷 20-17 ☆

● TSK
CCC
Terminal

● Hosyo
Roppongi

🐾 20-18 ●

🐾 20-10 ●

GAIEN HIGASHI DORI

Chaco
Steak
House ● 🚗 20-9 ☆

◉ 20-11 ☆
🐾 20-12
● 20-13 ☆

Hotel
Ibis ●

🐾 20-6 ☆ 🐾 20-7 ☆
🐾 20-8

🐾 20-19 ●
● Victoria

🐾 20-14 ● ● 🏢 20-15 ☆   🐾 20-16 ☆ ●

Books
Seishido ●

🐾 20-22 ●   🏢 20-24 ●   🐾 20-25 ●

Daiichi
Kangyo
Bank ●

🐾 20-23

RO
C

🏢 20-21 ☆ ●

TRACK 2 TO KAMIYACHO

Almond ●
🏢 20-28

ROPPONGI STA.
(Hibiya Line)

● Meidi-ya

Mitsui
Bank ●

TRACK 1 TO HIROO

Aoyama ●
Book   ● 20-26 ☆
Center

● 20-27

▼ Continued on Map No.21

Map No.20 Roppongi

20-1	1F	Koshi	▼	Nihon-ryori
20-2	1F	Torigin		Yakitori
20-3	1F	☆ Shirakawa	◉	Hida
20-4	1F	☆ Chisen		Kushi-age
20-5	1F	Naka		Yakitori
20-6	1F	☆ Chisen		Kushi-age
20-7	2F	☆ Tensho		Tempura
20-8	3F	Matsuri		Yakitori
20-9	3F	☆ Chako		Shabu-shabu
20-10	1F	Koami		Tonkatsu
20-11	B1	☆ Shin Miura	◉	Hakata-mizutaki
20-12	B1	Inagiku		Tempura
20-13	B1	☆ Otsuna-zushi		Sushi
20-14	2F	Kushinobo		Kushi-katsu
20-15	2F	☆ Honmura-an		Soba
20-16	1F	☆ Otsuna-zushi		Sushi
20-17	1F	☆ Daikan-kamado		Kani
20-18	B1	☆ Kamakura		Yakitori
20-19	1F	Yoshino		Sukiyaki
20-20	1F	Masuyoshi		Sushi
20-21	B1	☆ Koruza		Teppanyaki
20-22	1F	Sushisei		Sushi
20-23	1F	Torigin		Yakitori
20-24	2F	Konta		Iso-yaki
20-25	B1	Mentaro		Udon
20-26	B1	☆ Hassan		Shabu-shabu
20-27	1F	Sanshuya		Kappo
20-28	B1	Kobe 77		Teppanyaki

Map No.21 Roppongi

School

SHUTO EXPRESS WAY

Tampopo

21-8

21-11

21-7

21-4

21-3

Roppongi
Square Bldg.

21-10

21-5

Serina

21-2

21-6

Pub
Cardinal

Charleston

Cemetery

GAIEN HIGASHI DORI

Café
Bonpa

21-9

▲ Continued on Map No.20

Map No.21 Roppongi

21-1	1F	☆ Nanban-tei	🐔	Yakitori
21-2	B1	Shotaro	🍢	Kushi-age
21-3	3F	☆ Kushihachi	🐔	Yakitori
21-4	1F	Kabuto-ya	🍤	Sushi
21-5	1F	☆ Zoroku-zushi	🍤	Sushi
21-6	1F	☆ Seryna	🐂	Shabu-shabu
21-7	B1	Ippei	🍱	Oden
21-8	1F	☆ Chihei	🐟	Sakana
21-9	B1	☆ Fox-tail	🦀	Kani
21-10	1F	☆ Ajiman	🐡	Fugu

Map No.22 Shibuya

Tokyu Hands

22-6☆

22-2☆

Oak Village ●

Health Box ●

22-7☆

22-8

22-3☆

22-4☆

22-1 ☆

22-5

South Pacific

Grand Tokyo ●

Taiyo Kobe Bank

Iris Optical ●

22-29☆

22-30

22-9

22-10☆

22-11☆

22-12 Parc

22-13

22-14

22-15 Seit

Parco ●

Hotel Orient

22-18☆

Bingo In

Moncie ●

Fine

22-19☆

Pub Parco

22-20

22-21

Ponpa— dour ●

22-23

22-22

First Kitchen ●

22-24☆

212

▼Continued on Map No.24

Map No.22 Shibuya

22-1	1F	☆ Komagata Dojo	⊃ Dojo
22-2	1F	☆ Irifune	⊃ Unagi
22-3	1F	Kujira-ya	🐋 Kujira
22-4	B1	☆ Matsumae	◉ Hoppo
22-5	4F	Nagayamon	🦑 Nabe/anko
22-6	1F	☆ Tengu	🔥 Robatayaki
22-7	1F	☆ Kushisuke	🐔 Kushi-yaki
22-8	1F	Tappi	🥢 Kappo
22-9	3F	Kaike-tei	🍢 Kushi-age
22-10	8F	☆ Hyo-tei	🍱 Kaiseki
22-11	8F	☆ Inagiku	🍤 Tempura
22-12	6F	Kobe-ya	🐮 Shabu-shabu
22-13	7F	Konpira-ya	🍜 Soba
22-14	7F	Noto	◉ Hokuriku
22-15	7F	Sushiden	🐟 Sushi
22-16	7F	Teppo-ya	🍚 Kamameshi
22-17	7F	Toge	🍜 Soba
22-18	B1	☆ Kushinobo	🍢 Kushi-katsu
22-19	B1	☆ Koyasu	🍤 Tempura
22-20	B1	Nagayamon	🔥 Robatayaki
22-21	1F	Kiraku-zushi	🐟 Sushi
22-22	4F	Tarafuku	🔥 Robatayaki
22-23	B1	Saga	🔥 Robatayaki
22-24	1F	☆ Yamabuki	⊃ Unagi
22-25	1F	☆ Gin-tei	🐡 Fugu/nabe
22-26	2F	Isogen	🥢 Kappo
22-27	1F	Midori	🥢 Kappo
22-28	7F	☆ Uemura	🍱 Kaiseki
22-29	B1	☆ Kani-ya	🦀 Kani
22-30	1F	Kujira-ya	🐋 Kujira

▶Continued on Map No.23

| 22 | 23 |
| 24 | 25 | 26 | Shibuya Sta. — Map Nos. 24, 25

Map No.23 Shibuya

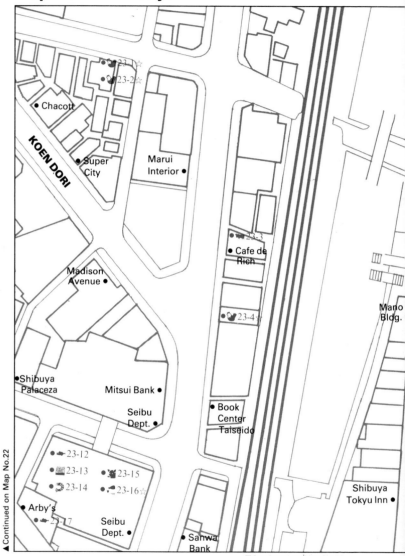

◀ Continued on Map No.22

▼Continued on Map No.25

Map No.23 Shibuya

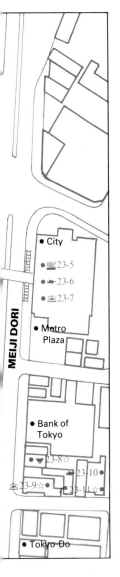

23-1	1F	☆	Hida Takayama	Kushi-yaki
23-2	1F	☆	Rowaru	Kushi-yaki
23-3	2F		Suehiro	Shabu-shabu
23-4	2F	☆	Nanban-tei	Yakitori
23-5	1F		Maru-ya	Soba
23-6	2F		Rokube-sushi	Sushi
23-7	2F		Tsuta	Robatayaki
23-8	2F	☆	Hayashi	Kisetsu
23-9	3F	☆	Funabenkei	Robatayaki
23-10	B2		Matsu-ya	Sakana
23-11	2F	☆	Saruyama	Kappo
23-12	8F		Kuruma-zushi	Sushi
23-13	8F		Yabuizu	Soba
23-14	8F		Tenichi	Tempura
23-15	8F		Ton-tei	Tonkatsu
23-16	8F	☆	Uemura	Kappo
23-17	2F		Irori	Sushi

22 23
24 25 26 Shibuya Sta.—Map Nos. 24, 25

Map No.24 Shibuya

▲Continued on Map No.22

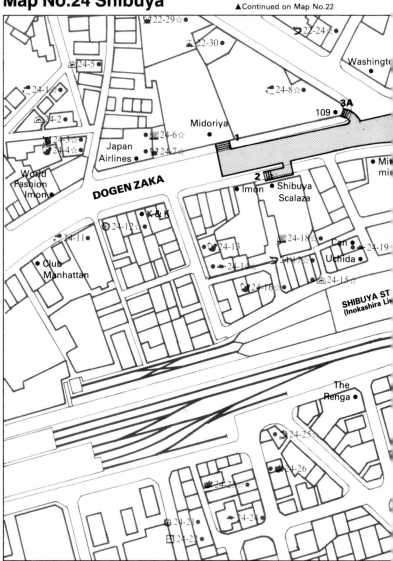

22-29☆
22-24☆
22-30
Washington
24-5
24-8☆
24-1☆
3A
109
24-2
Midoriya
1
24-6☆
24-3☆
Japan
24-7☆
Mi
24-4☆
Airlines
mi
World
2
Fashion
Imon
Imon
Shibuya
Scalaza
DOGEN ZAKA
K & K
24-12
24-11
24-18☆
Can
24-19
24-13
Uchida
Club
24-17☆
Manhattan
24-14
SHIBUYA ST
24-16☆
24-15☆
(Inokashira Li

The
Renga
24-25☆
24-26
24-24
24-20
24-24
24-21
24-23

Map No.24 Shibuya

24-1	1F	☆	Goen-tei	⚑ Kappo
24-2	2F		Hokkai	🏮 Robatayaki
24-3	1F	☆	Katsuichi	🐖 Tonkatsu
24-4	B1	☆	Kushisuke	🐦 Kushi-yaki
24-5	3F		Furusato	🏮 Robatayaki
24-6	5F	☆	Izumo	🍜 Udon
24-7	8F	☆	Kanitani	🦀 Kani
24-8	1F	☆	Tamakyu	⚑ Kappo
24-9	6F	☆	Tsunahachi	🍤 Tempura
24-10	1F	☆	Matsukawa	🐟 Unagi
24-11	1F		Maruhachi	⚑ Kappo
24-12	3F	☆	Ohotsuku	◉ Hokkaido
24-13	1F		Torimasu	🐦 Yakitori
24-14	1F	☆	Sushifumi	🍤 Sushi
24-15	1F	☆	Inaka	🏮 Robatayaki
24-16	1F	☆	Sasameyuki	🐦 Yakitori
24-17	1F	☆	Unatetsu	🐟 Unagi
24-18	1F	☆	Tanima	🍜 Udon
24-19	1F	☆	Yanagi-zushi	🍤 Sushi
24-20	1F		Yakitori Kaikan	🐦 Yakitori
24-21	B1		Tanikaze	🍲 Chanko-nabe
24-22	B1		Tsugi	🍢 Oden
24-23	1F	☆	Tsukiji	🐡 Fugu
24-24	1F		Otsuna-zushi	🍤 Sushi
24-25	1F	☆	Tenmatsu	🍤 Tempura
24-26	1F		Tsukada	🐡 Fugu

▼Continued on Map No.25

22 | 23
24 | 25 | 26   Shibuya Sta. — Map Nos. 24, 25

Map No.25 Shibuya

▲Continued on Map No.23

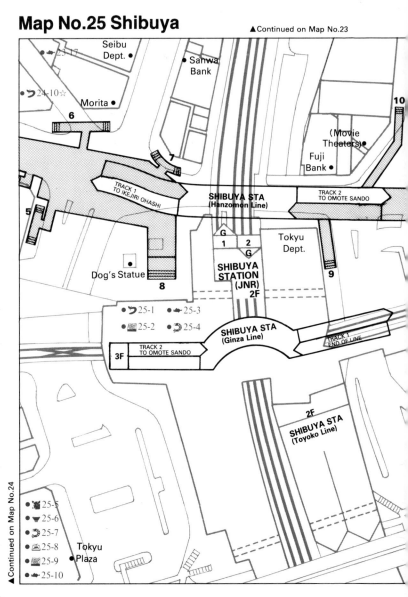

Seibu Dept. ●

● 25-17

● Sanwa Bank

● 24-10☆

Morita ●

6

7

TRACK 1
TO IKEJIRI OHASHI

5

10

(Movie Theaters)●

Fuji Bank ●

SHIBUYA STA
(Hanzomon Line)

TRACK 2
TO OMOTE SANDO

G
1 2
G

Tokyu Dept.

9

● Dog's Statue

8

SHIBUYA STATION (JNR)
2F

● 25-1   ● 25-3
● 25-2   ● 25-4

SHIBUYA STA
(Ginza Line)

TRACK 1
END OF LINE

3F   TRACK 2
TO OMOTE SANDO

2F
SHIBUYA STA
(Toyoko Line)

▲Continued on Map No.24

● 25-5
● 25-6
● 25-7
● 25-8
● 25-9
● 25-10

Tokyu Plaza

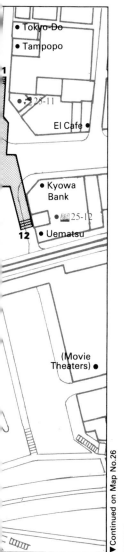

Map No.25 Shibuya

25-1	8F	Hoshigaoka-saryo	🌀 Unagi
25-2	8F	Namiki	🍜 Soba
25-3	8F	Sushibun	🍤 Sushi
25-4	8F	Tenmatsu	🍤 Tempura
25-5	9F	Horai-tei	🍖 Tonkatsu
25-6	9F	Iraka	🐟 Kansai-ryori
25-7	9F	Matsukawa	🍤 Tempura
25-8	9F	Ta-ya	🐟 Sakana
25-9	B2	Kazoku-tei	🍜 Soba
25-10	9F	Tama-zushi	🍤 Sushi
25-11	B1	Nanahan	🍢 Kappo
25-12	1F	Fuku-ya	🍜 Soba

▶ Continued on Map No.26

Shibuya Sta. — Map Nos. 24, 25

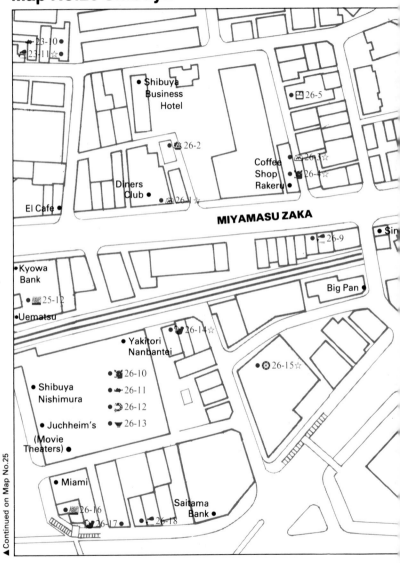

23-10
23-11☆

● Shibuya
Business
Hotel

🏠 26-5

🏢 26-2

Coffee
Shop
Rakeru ●

26-3 ☆
26-4 ☆

Diners
Club ●

🏢 26-1 ☆

El Café ●

MIYAMASU ZAKA

26-9

● Sin

● Kyowa
Bank

Big Pan ●

● 🏢 25-12

●Uematsu

26-14 ☆

● Yakitori
Nanbantei

◉ 26-15 ☆

🏢 26-10

● Shibuya
Nishimura

26-11

🐷 26-12

● Juchheim's

26-13

(Movie
Theaters) ●

◀ Continued on Map No.25

● Miami

Saitama
Bank ●

🏢 26-16

26-17

26-18

Map No.26 Shibuya

26-1	B1	☆ Isochu	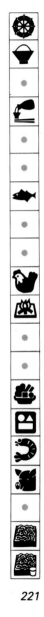 Nishin-ryori
26-2	B1	Hachiga	Sakura-nabe
26-3	1F	☆ Michinoku	Sankai-ryori
26-4	1F	☆ Miyamasu-tei	Tonkatsu
26-5	1F	Wakashiro	Oden
26-6	1F	☆ Chotoku	Te-uchi
26-7	1F	Sawanoi	Udon
26-8	B1	☆ Masa	Kappo
26-9	B1	Kumamoto-ya	Kappo
26-10	4F	Kaika-tei	Tonkatsu
26-11	4F	Kiku-zushi	Sushi
26-12	4F	Tenkin	Tempura
26-13	4F	Yakura	Washoku
26-14	1F	☆ Nanban-tei	Yakitori
26-15	2F	☆ Neboke	Tosa
26-16	B1	Shogetsu-an	Soba
26-17	1F	Kappa-do	Yakitori
26-18	B1	Kiku	Kappo

22	23	
24	25	**26**

Shibuya Sta. — Map Nos. 24, 25

Map No.27 Shimbashi

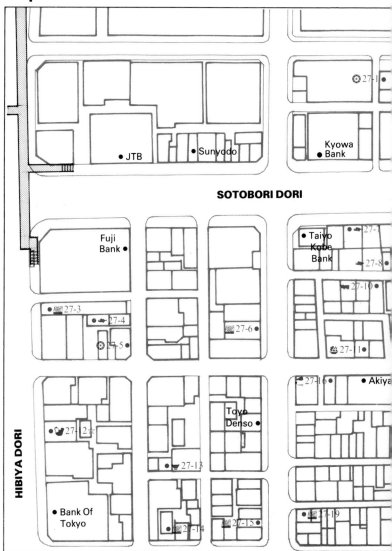

Map No.27 Shimbashi

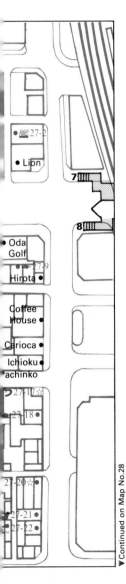

27-1	B1	Ajikine	⚙ Hakata
27-2	1F	Choju-an	🍜 Soba
27-3	1F	Sarashina	🍜 Soba
27-4	1F	Fuku-zushi	🍤 Sushi
27-5	1F	Satsuma-shamo	⚙ Kagoshima
27-6	1F	Mimiu	🍜 Udon
27-7	1F	Shinoda-zushi	🍤 Sushi
27-8	1F	Ko-ume	🍤 Sushi
27-9	1F	Wakana	🍤 Sushi
27-10	1F	Cho-ya	🐔 Mizutaki
27-11	1F	Hatsufuji	🦐 Nabe
27-12	1F	☆ Torishige	🐔 Tori-kappo
27-13	1F	Kamome	🐟 Ko-ryori
27-14	1F	Maruga	🍜 Soba
27-15	1F	Shogetsu-an	🍜 Soba
27-16	1F	Edogin	🍱 Edo-kappo
27-17	1F	☆ Owada Honten	🍢 Unagi
27-18	1F	Daiwa-zushi	🍤 Sushi
27-19	1F	Rengyu-an	🍜 Soba
27-20	1F	☆ Su-egen	🍱 Kappo
27-21	1F	Torigin	🐔 Yakitori
27-22	1F	Kuruma-zushi	🍱 Kappo

▶ Continued on Map No.28

27 | 28 Shimbashi Sta.—Map No. 28

223

Map No.28 Shimbashi

Jujin Plaza

28-1

28-2

28-3

Daiwa Bank

5

SHIMBASHI STA
(Ginza Line)

TRACK 2 TO GINZA

TRACK 1 TO TORANOMON

7

8

6

4

Meiji Daisy

(Steam Locomotive)

(Water Fountain)

SHIMBASHI STATION (JNR)

Uts

T 2 1 T
B G 3 G B
6 5 4

Pachinko Toyota

28-5

28-6   28-9

28-7   28-10

28-8   28-11

▲ Continued on Map No.27

Map No.28 Shimbashi

28-1	1F	Nobori-tei	⮑	Unagi
28-2	2F	Wakatake	▼	Nihon-ryori
28-3	1F	Daimonji	🎴	Okonomiyaki
28-4	1F	Kinbei	🐟	Sushi
28-5	B1	Deyohai	🦎	Suppon/turtle
28-6	B1	Fukuju	🎴	Okonomiyaki
28-7	4F	Funaosa	🐟	Sashimi
28-8	B1	Kawa	🐷	Tonkatsu
28-9	4F	Kazumura	🐷	Tonkatsu
28-10	B1	Tojinbo	⊙	Hokuriku
28-11	4F	Yukku	⊙	Hokkaido

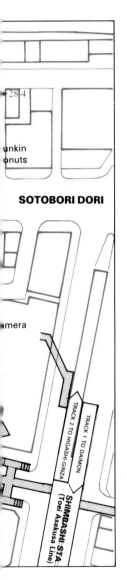

SOTOBORI DORI

unkin
onuts

amera

TRACK 2 TO HIGASHI-GINZA
TRACK 1 TO DAIMON

SHIMBASHI STA.
(Toei Asakusa Line)

28-4

Map No.29 Shinjuku

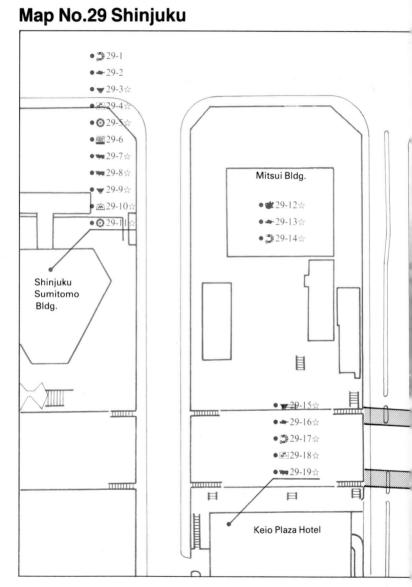

- 🦐 29-1
- 🍜 29-2
- 🍷 29-3☆
- 📷 29-4☆
- ⚙ 29-5☆
- 🍱 29-6
- 🍴 29-7☆
- 🍴 29-8☆
- 🍷 29-9☆
- 🏯 29-10☆
- ⚙ 29-11☆

Shinjuku
Sumitomo
Bldg.

Mitsui Bldg.

- 🍰 29-12☆
- 🍜 29-13☆
- 🦐 29-14☆

- 🍷 29-15☆
- 🍜 29-16☆
- 🦐 29-17☆
- 📷 29-18☆
- 🍴 29-19☆

Keio Plaza Hotel

Map No.29 Shinjuku

29-1	49F	Donto	Tempura
29-2	50F	Kanihachi	Sushi
29-3	51F	☆ Koshikijima	Wafu
29-4	48F	☆ Minokichi	Kyo-ryori
29-5	50F	☆ Neboke	Tosa
29-6	50F	Ranmen	Soba
29-7	50F	☆ Sanriba	Shabu-shabu
29-8	52F	☆ Seryna	Shabu-shabu
29-9	50F	☆ Seto-uchi	Washoku
29-10	49F	☆ Tarugen	Robatayaki
29-11	50F	☆ Yukku	Hokkaido
29-12	B1	☆ Kikumi	Fugu/kappo
29-13	B1	☆ Sushita	Sushi
29-14	B1	☆ Tenichi	Tempura
29-15	2F	☆ Ashibi	Nihon-ryori
29-16	7F	☆ Kyube	Sushi
29-17	7F	☆ Inagiku	Tempura
29-18	45F	☆ Miyama	Kaiseki
29-19	7F	☆ Okahan	Sukiyaki

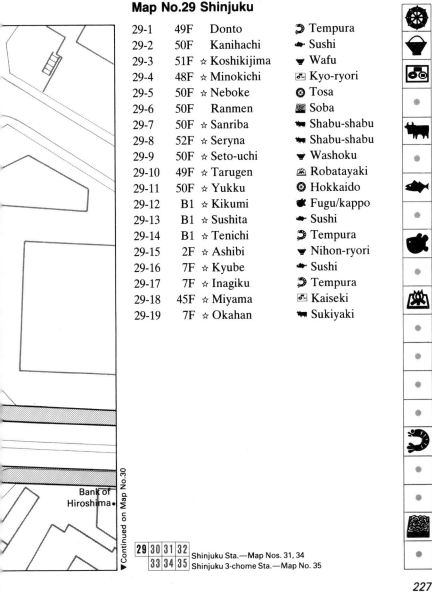

Bank of
Hiroshima●

◄ Continued on Map No.30

29 30 31 32
33 34 35
Shinjuku Sta.—Map Nos. 31, 34
Shinjuku 3-chome Sta.—Map No. 35

Map No.30 Shinjuku

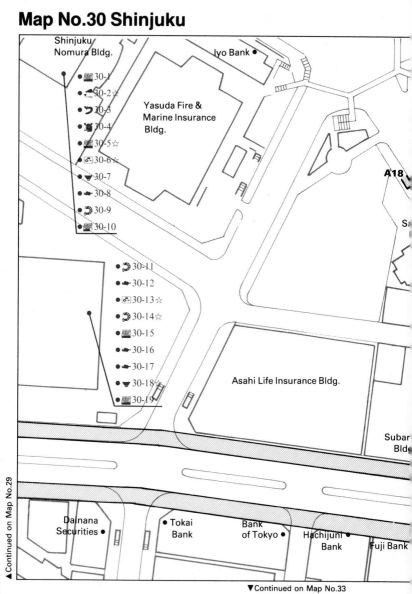

Shinjuku Nomura Bldg.

Iyo Bank ●

Yasuda Fire & Marine Insurance Bldg.

● 30-1
● 30-2☆
● 30-3
● 30-4
● 30-5☆
● 30-6☆
● 30-7
● 30-8
● 30-9
● 30-10

A18

S

● 30-11
● 30-12
● 30-13☆
● 30-14☆
● 30-15
● 30-16
● 30-17
● 30-18
● 30-19

Asahi Life Insurance Bldg.

Subar Bld

Dainana Securities ●

● Tokai Bank

Bank of Tokyo ●

Hachijuni ● Bank

Fuji Bank

◀ Continued on Map No.29

▼Continued on Map No.33

228

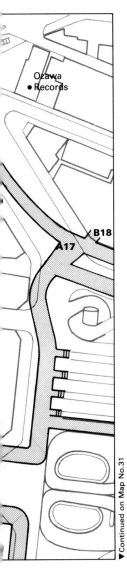

Map No.30 Shinjuku

30-1	49F	Miyoi-tei	Ramen
30-2	49F	☆ Ginsa-an	Kappo
30-3	B2	Haibara	Unagi
30-4	B2	Ise	Tonkatsu
30-5	B2	☆ Ranmen	Soba
30-6	B2	☆ Shimogamosaryo	Kyo-ryori
30-7	50F	Suigei-tei	Nihon-ryori
30-8	B2	Sushita	Sushi
30-9	49F	Tsunahachi	Tempura
30-10	49F	Usu-ya	Te-uchi
30-11	B1	Funabashi-ya	Tempura
30-12	B1	Kyotaru	Sushi
30-13	B1	☆ Kyoizumo-ya	Kaiseki
30-14	B1	☆ Minafuji	Tempura
30-15	B1	Ranmen	Soba
30-16	B1	Sharaku	Sushi
30-17	53F	Tama-zushi	Sushi
30-18	53F	☆ Tsukiji Uemura	Nihon-ryori
30-19	B1	Usu-ya	Udon

▼ Continued on Map No.31

29	30	31	32
33	34	35	

Shinjuku Sta.—Map Nos. 31, 34
Shinjuku 3-chome Sta.—Map No. 35

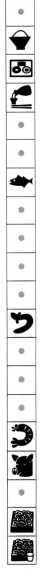

Map No. 31 Shinjuku

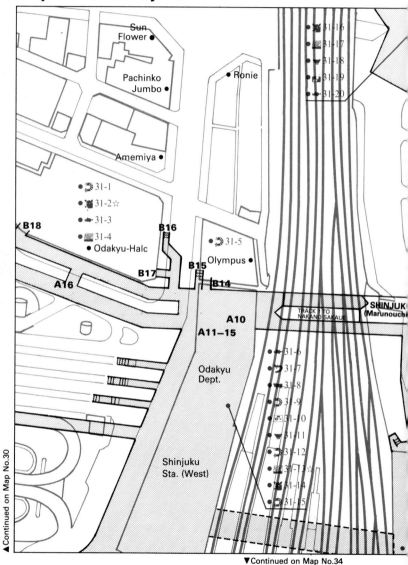

Sun Flower ●

Pachinko Jumbo ●

● Ronie

Amemiya ●

● 🐟 31-1
● 🍶 31-2 ☆
● 🦐 31-3
● 🍱 31-4
● Odakyu-Halc

● 🐟 31-5

Olympus ●

B18
B16
B17
B15
B14
A16
A10
A11–15

Odakyu Dept.

Shinjuku Sta. (West)

● 31-6
● 31-7
● 31-8
● 31-9
● 31-10
● 31-11
● 31-12
● 31-13 ☆
● 31-14
● 31-15

● 31-16
● 31-17
● 31-18
● 31-19
● 31-20

TRACK 1 TO NAKANO SAKAUE

SHINJUKU (Marunouchi

▲Continued on Map No.30

▼Continued on Map No.34

Map No.31 Shinjuku

31-1	B3	Hageten	Tempura
31-2	B3	☆ Katsukushi	Kushi-age
31-3	B3	Mikaku-zushi	Sushi
31-4	B3	Yamaga Soba	Soba
31-5	3F	Yamato	Tempura
31-6	10F	Fukusuke	Sushi
31-7	10F	Futaba	Unagi
31-8	10F	Gyu-ya	Sukiyaki
31-9	10F	Kinumaki	Tempura
31-10	10F	Kyunocha-ya	Kyo-ryori
31-11	9F	Manazuru	Nihon-ryori
31-12	B1	Tsunahachi	Tempura
31-13	10F	☆ Umemoto	Soba
31-14	10F	Wako	Tonkatsu
31-15	10F	Yakura	Tempura
31-16	B1	Danshaku	Tonkatsu
31-17	B1	Hanabishi	Udon
31-18	B1	Matsunobori	Nihon-ryori
31-19	B1	Tonju	Okonomiyaki
31-20	B1	Wakana	Sushi
31-21	1F	Ibuki	Sukiyaki
31-22	1F	Daikoku-ya	Shabu-shabu

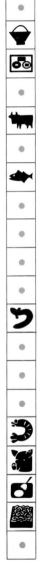

▼ Continued on Map No.32

29	30	31	32
33	34	35	

Shinjuku Sta. — Map Nos. 31, 34
Shinjuku 3-chome Sta. — Map No. 35

Map No.32 Shinjuku

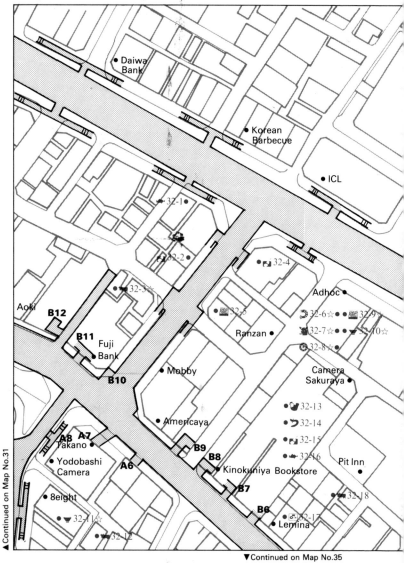

Daiwa Bank

Korean Barbecue

ICL

32-1

32-2

32-4

32-3☆

Adhoc

Aoki

B12

32-5

32-6☆ 32-9☆

Ranzan

32-7☆ 32-10☆

B11

Fuji Bank

32-8☆

Camera Sakuraya

B10

Mobby

32-13

Americaya

32-14

32-15

A8 A7

Takano

32-16

Pit Inn

A6

Yodobashi Camera

B9

B8

Kinokuniya Bookstore

B7

8eight

B6

32-18

32-11☆

32-17

Lemina

32-12

▲Continued on Map No.31

▼Continued on Map No.35

Map No.32 Shinjuku

32-1	1F	Ogi-zushi	Sushi
32-2	3F	Pasu-takan	Okonomiyaki
32-3	1F	☆ Kobayashi	Sukiyaki
32-4	4F	Yochan	Okonomiyaki
32-5	1F	Kuruma-ya	Udon
32-6	3F	☆ Hageten	Tempura
32-7	3F	☆ Kushinobo	Kushi-katsu
32-8	8F	☆ Shamo	Satsuma
32-9	8F	☆ Uta-andon	Soba
32-10	B1	☆ Yoigokoro	Nihon-ryori
32-11	5F	☆ Fune	Nihon-ryori
32-12	1F	Bajohai	Shabu-shabu
32-13	B1	Sho-ya	Kushi-yaki
32-14	B1	Takabe	Unagi
32-15	B1	Tonkichi	Okonomiyaki
32-16	1F	Ageha-zushi	Sushi
32-17	1F	Tagawa	Kaiseki/fugu
32-18	7F	Yasube	Shabu-shabu

YASUKUNI DORI

Isetan Kaikan •

Isetan Dept.

29 30 31 **32**
33 34 35

Shinjuku Sta.—Map Nos. 31, 34
Shinjuku 3-chome Sta.—Map No. 35

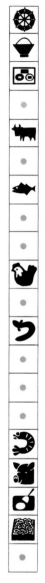

Map No.33 Shinjuku

▲Continued on Map No.30

Yasuda Mutual Life Insurance

● Takakura Bldg.

Kadoya Hotel ●

🚩 33-1☆

AIU ●

● Chinese Restaurant

Takakura Bldg. ●

● Steak House

🍎 33-2

● Gekkoso Shinjuku

● Art Shop Sekaido

● Hokkaidō Bank

All Nippon Airways ●

Yodobashi Camera ●

● Town West Bldg.

Seiko Chinese Restaurant ●

Saitama Bank ●

● Toyota

● Golf Shop

● Condor

Fuji Xerox ●

🏯 33-5☆

● Camera Doi

● JCI

Salem ●

Kinki Nippon Tourist ●

Kit

Meiho Bldg. ●

● Aladdin

🚩 33-6

⊚ 33-7

Map No.33 Shinjuku

33-1	1F	☆ Imasa	▼ Kisetsu
33-2	1F	Matahei	🦪 Fugu
33-3	B2	Futaba	🐗 Shabu-shabu
33-4	B1	Yanagi-zushi	🐟 Sushi
33-5	B1	☆ Isohama	🏔 Sakana
33-6	B1	Misono-zushi	🐟 Sushi
33-7	B1	Hyuga	◉ Miyazaki

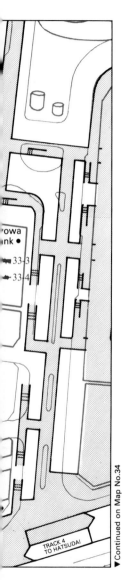

▼ Continued on Map No.34

29 30 31 32
33 34 35
Shinjuku Sta.—Map Nos. 31, 34
Shinjuku 3-chome Sta.—Map No. 35

Map No.34 Shinjuku

▲Continued on Map No.31

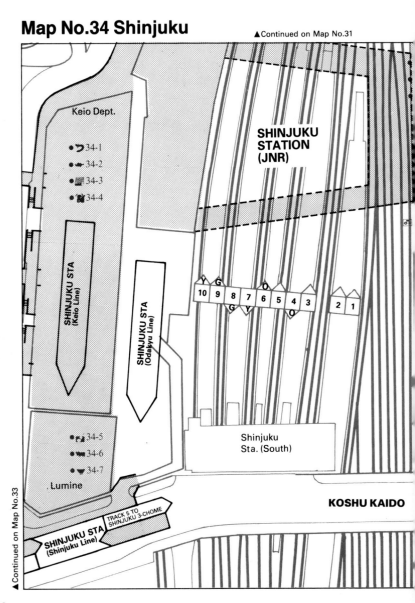

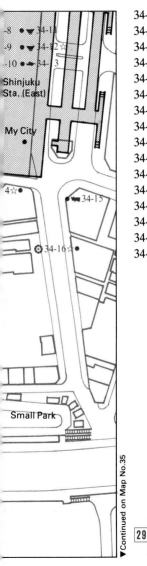

Map No.34 Shinjuku

34-1	B1	Futaba	🌀 Unagi
34-2	B1	Kyotaru	🍤 Sushi
34-3	8F	Sanki	🍜 Te-uchi
34-4	B1	Tonkichi	🍢 Teppanyaki
34-5	6F	Boteju	🍳 Okonomiyaki
34-6	6F	Imahan	🐂 Sukiyaki
34-7	6F	Keyaki	🐟 Kisetsu
34-8	7F	Funabashi-ya	🦐 Tempura
34-9	7F	Hamada-ya	🐟 Nihon-ryori
34-10	7F	Izumi	🦐 Tempura
34-11	7F	Kitahama	🐟 Kansai-ryori
34-12	8F	☆ Matsuzumi	🐟 Kisetsu
34-13	7F	Wakana	🍤 Sushi
34-14	6F	☆ Kakiden	🍱 Kyo-kaiseki
34-15	9F	Suehiro	🐂 Sukiyaki
34-16	B1	☆ Kurawanka	◎ Kagoshima

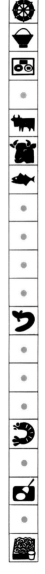

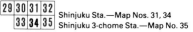

Shinjuku Sta.—Map Nos. 31, 34
Shinjuku 3-chome Sta.—Map No. 35

▼Continued on Map No.35

237

Map No.35 Shinjuku

▲Continued on Map No.32

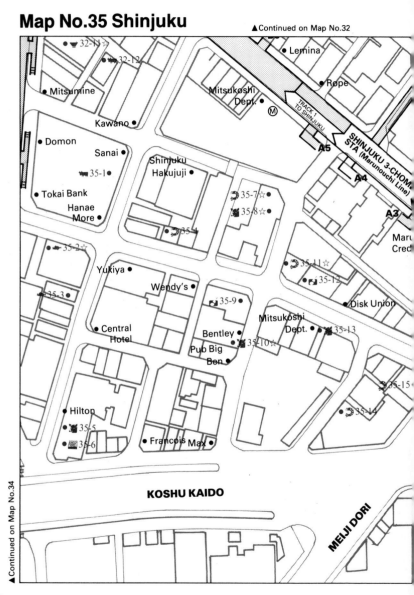

▲Continued on Map No.34

Map No.35 Shinjuku

35-1	B2	Mawarikoma	🐄 Sukiyaki
35-2	1F	☆ Tamagawa-zushi	🍤 Sushi
35-3	1F	Ogi-zushi	🍤 Sushi
35-4	1F	Tsunahachi	🍤 Tempura
35-5	1F	Katsu-tei	🐷 Tonkatsu
35-6	2F	Sarashina	🍜 Soba
35-7	1F	☆ Funabashi-ya	🍤 Tempura
35-8	1F	☆ Tonton-tei	🐷 Tonkatsu
35-9	1F	Hyakka	🍳 Okonomiyaki
35-10	5F	☆ Tachikichi	🐷 Kushi-age
35-11	1F	☆ Tsunahachi	🍤 Tempura
35-12	2F	Tanuki	🍳 Okonomiyaki
35-13	1F	Santa	🐷 Tonkatsu
35-14	1F	Masuda-ya	🍤 Tempura
35-15	B2	Tenmatsu	🍤 Tempura
35-16	B1	Hitokuchi	🍲 Washoku
35-17	B1	Kiyoshi	🍲 Nihon-ryori
35-18	B1	☆ Kyocha-ya	🍤 Sushi
35-19	B1	Shinano	🍜 Soba
35-20	7F	Shiwano	🍜 Soba
35-21	B1	Tonju	🍳 Okonomiyaki
35-22	7F	Wakamatsu	🍚 Kamameshi

29 30 31 32
33 34 35
Shinjuku Sta.—Map Nos. 31, 34
Shinjuku 3-chome Sta.—Map No. 35

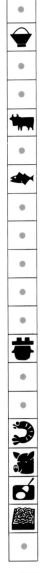

Map No.36 Tsukiji

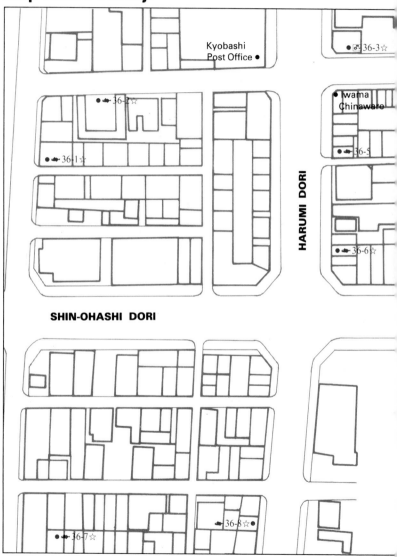

Kyobashi
Post Office ●

● 36-3☆

● Iwama
Chinaware

● 36-2☆

● 36-5

● 36-1☆

HARUMI DORI

● 36-6☆

SHIN-OHASHI DORI

36-8☆●

● 36-7☆

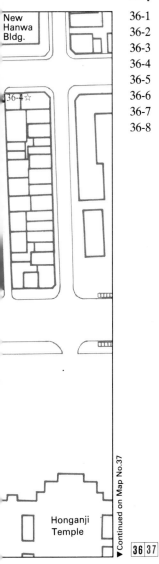

New
Hanwa
Bldg.

36-4 ☆

Honganji
Temple

▼ Continued on Map No.37

36|**37**

Map No.36 Tsukiji

36-1	1F	☆ Edogin	➤ Sushi
36-2	1F	☆ Chikara-zushi	➤ Sushi
36-3	1F	☆ Uemura	⬛ Kaiseki
36-4	1F	☆ Sarashina	▦ Soba
36-5	1F	Echigo-zushi	➤ Sushi
36-6	1F	☆ Sushi-iwa	➤ Sushi
36-7	1F	☆ Sushisei	➤ Sushi
36-8	1F	☆ Kiraku-zushi	➤ Sushi

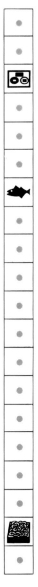

Map No. 37 Tsukiji

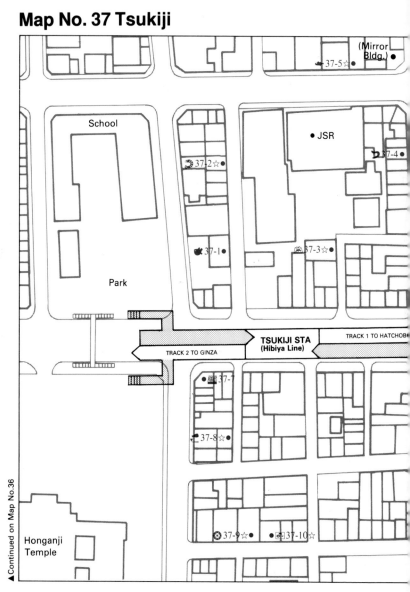

(Mirror Bldg.) ●
37-5 ☆ ●

School

● JSR

37-2 ☆ ●

37-4 ●

37-1 ●

37-3 ☆ ●

Park

TSUKIJI STA
(Hibiya Line)

TRACK 1 TO HATCHOB

TRACK 2 TO GINZA

● 37-7

37-8 ☆ ●

Continued on Map No.36

Honganji
Temple

37-9 ☆ ●

● 37-10 ☆

◀Continued on Map No.36

Map No.37 Tsukiji

37-1	B1	Senami		Fugu
37-2	1F	☆ Okame		Tempura
37-3	1F	☆ Hida		Robatayaki
37-4	1F	Miyagawa		Unagi
37-5	1F	☆ Tama-zushi Honten		Sushi
37-6	1F	☆ Miyagawa Honten		Unagi
37-7	1F	Kose-an		Soba
37-8	1F	☆ Nakata		Kappo
37-9	1F	☆ Yoshimoto		Tosa
37-10	1F	☆ Takano		Kaiseki

SHIN-OHASHI DORI

36 37 Tsukiji Sta.—Map No. 37

243

Map No.38 Ueno

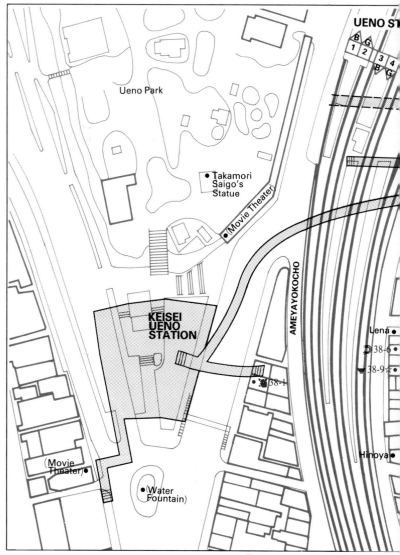

UENO ST

B G
1 2 3 4
B G

Ueno Park

• Takamori Saigo's Statue

Movie Theater

• Movie Theater

AMEYA YOKOCHO

KEISEI UENO STATION

Lena •

38-6 •

38-9 •

38-1 •

Hinoya •

(Movie Theater) •

• (Water Fountain)

Map No.38 Ueno

38-1	2F	Masuhisa		Tonkatsu
38-2	1F	☆ Santomo		Ikizukuri
38-3	5F	Saberi		Ko-ryori
38-4	4F	Benkei-zushi		Sushi
38-5	1F	Shinsei		Oden
38-6	1F	Suigetsu		Tempura
38-7	1F	Maruhachi		Tempura
38-8	1F	Kani-ya Honten		Kani
38-9	1F	☆ Takebun		Kisetsu
38-10	1F	Janome-zushi		Sushi
38-11	6F	Santomo		Unagi
38-12	6F	Yabu Soba		Soba
38-13	6F	Ao-yagi		Sushi
38-14	1F	☆ Yabu Soba		Soba

38 Okachimachi Sta.—Map No. 39
39 Ueno Sta.—Map No. 38

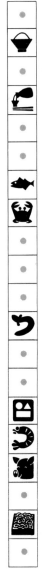

Map No.39 Ueno

▲Continued on Map No.38

(Water Fountain)

39-7☆
39-8

39-11
39-12
39-9☆
39-10☆
39-13
Plaza・U

39-1☆

39-2

Trumps

Kameido
39-14☆

Optique
Hakusan●

39-3☆

39-4
39-5☆

Marumiya

39-15 ● Mitsumine

39-6

Suzuya

39-16

39-18

Hatoya

39-17

39-19☆ Lotteria ●

CHUO DORI

UENO NAKA DORI

UENO NAKA DORI

KASUGA DORI

Map No.39 Ueno

39-1	1F	☆ Izuei	𝄢	Unagi
39-2	1F	Rengyoku-an	🍲	Soba
39-3	1F	☆ Futaba	🍖	Tonkatsu
39-4	1F	Tensuzu	🍤	Tempura
39-5	1F	☆ Honmoku-tei	🍶	Nihon-ryori
39-6	1F	Gomangoku	🍣	Sushi
39-7	1F	☆ Kamameshi Haru	🍚	Kamameshi
39-8	1F	Taimaru	🍤	Tempura
39-9	5F	☆ Tsunamachi	🍤	Tempura
39-10	5F	☆ Uemura	🥢	Kappo
39-11	1F	Kappa-zushi	🍣	Sushi
39-12	1F	Matsuei-zushi	🍣	Sushi
39-13	1F	Taimaru	🍖	Tonkatsu
39-14	1F	☆ Benkei	𝄢	Unagi
39-15	1F	Genji	🍣	Sushi ·
39-16	1F	Tonhachi-tei	🍖	Tonkatsu
39-17	1F	Futaba	🍖	Tonkatsu
39-18	1F	Kappa-zushi	🍣	Sushi
39-19	1F	☆ Mansei-an	🍲	Kishimen
39-20	1F	☆ Tarumatsu	🔥	Robatayaki
39-21	1F	Irori	🔥	Robatayaki
39-22	6F	Yanagawa Kaikan	🍳	Okonomiyaki

38 Okachimachi Sta. — Map No. 39
39 Ueno Sta. — Map No. 38

● Japan's National Drink:
Sake

The specialty of a bartender I used to know at a Japanese restaurant in Boston was "*sake* martinis"— using *sake* instead of vermouth and a cucumber slice instead of an olive. With this delightfully fresh concoction, he claimed it was easy to wean diehard cocktail drinkers onto pure *sake*.

Sake (pronounced sah-kay), is the national spirits of Japan. It is also called *nihon-shu*. Although clear like vodka, *sake* is smoother, sweeter and usually is served hot, rather than on the rocks. A sweet heavy-tasting variety of *sake* with a high alcohol content is an indispensable kitchen seasoning (*mirin*).

Japanese *sake* and food are often served together. At any drinking establishment (*nomiya*), one will find an infinite list of grilled, stewed, boiled, and otherwise prepared dishes such as vinagrettes, which are served as hors d'oeuvres with *sake*. The two specialty restaurants which cater especially to *sake* drinkers are *yakitori-ya* and *robatayaki-ya* (see pages 85 and 91 respectively).

●
History of Sake

Sake plays a part in Japan's earliest legends and is used in many religious ceremonies. In a *Shinto* wedding ceremony, for instance, the marriage is sealed by the exchange of cups of *sake*. To bring good luck at the New Year, family members share cups of a variety of *sake* (*toso*) which is steeped with medicinal herbs.

Sake is 7–9 percent proof, and thus is slightly more potent than wine. It is a fermented beverage which takes 45 to 60 days to produce.

Sake uses the traditional Japanese unit of measure, the "*go*" which is equivalent to 180 milliliters or about 6.09 ounces. The typical *sake* bottle is about half a gallon, which conveniently contains 10 "*go*" (1.8 liters). The *sake* flask contains a more reasonable drinking quantity, one "*go*." To the best of our knowledge, the phrase "to have a go of it" did not enter the English language from Japanese.

Gourmet Tips

Unlike wine, *sake* doesn't improve with age, so always drink the latest vintage. *Sake* is optimally served slightly warmer than body temperature. Heating *sake* seems to make it quite a bit more volitile and the vapors certainly to go right to the head. However, cold *sake* is also imbibed, by the glass (*koppu*) or in small square cedar boxes (*masuzake*) with a pinch of salt in one corner like tequila, to bring out the sweetness.

Sake comes in three grades—top, first class and second class (*tokkyu*, *ikkyu* and *nikyu*)—and two varieties—dry and sweet (*karakuchi* and *amakuchi*). The best waters for brewing *sake* are said to be from the Nada area of Hyogo near Kobe and Fushimi in Kyoto.

Drinking Bouts

Since the pub is primarily the Japanese man's domain, it is possible for those who are willing to engage in drinking bouts to achieve quickly a form of non-verbal rapport the Japanese call *su-kin-shippu* ("skinship"). "Skinship," coined form the words "kinship" and "skin," is a term used to describe the sort of visceral communication among the members of a family. It is the hearty elbow-rubbing of drinking companions which leads to mutual understanding.

Not merely getting drunk, but the ettiquite of drink-pouring itself facilitates "skinship"—the emphasis being to anticipate and provide for the other's needs. Unlike Westerners, however, who consider it rude to be plied with liquor if they don't wish to get drunk, the Japanese always make the friendly gesture of accepting a friendly overture in the spirit of the occasion.

▲ *Sake* bottle and typical service

● Glossary of Japanese Food Words

MEATS

Bacon	*Beekon*
Beef (see P.46)	*Gyu niku, Beefu*
Chicken (see P.79)	*Tori niku*
Duck	*Kamo, Ahiru*
Egg	*Tamago*
Fillet	*Hi-re*
Fish	*Sakana*
Froglegs	*Shokuyo gaeru*
Ham	*Hamu*
Hamburger, deep-fried	*Menchi katsu*
Horsemeat	*Ba niku*
Lamb	*Ramu*
Liver	*Rebaa*
Marbled choice beef	*Shimofuri niku*
Meat	*Niku*
Meatballs, grilled	*Tsukune*
Mutton	*Maton*
Pork	*Buta niku, Pooku*
Quail	*Uzura*
Rabbit	*Usagi*
Sparrow	*Suzume*
Steak	*Suteeki (Saaroin, Tendaaroin)*
Turkey	*Shichi mencho*
Turtle, Terrapin	*Suppon*
Veal	*Koushi*
Venison	*Shika niku*
Wild boar	*Inoshishi*

SEAFOODS

Abalone	*Awabi*
Angler fish	*Anko*
Ark shell	*Akagai*
Blue-fin tuna	*Kuro maguro*
Blue fusilier	*Aodai*
Bonito, Skipjack tuna	*Katsuo*
Carp	*Koi*
Catfish	*Namazu*
Clam	*Hamaguri, Asari*
Cod	*Tara*
Cod roe	*Tarako*
Conch shell	*Sazae*
Crab	*Kani*
Cutlass fish	*Tachi-uo*
Eel (see P.92)	*Unagi*
Fish	*Sakana*
Flounder, Sole	*Hirame*
Herring	*Nishin*
Horse mackerel	*Ma-aji*
Jellyfish	*Kurage*
King Crab	*Taraba gani*
Loach (see P.98)	*Dojo*
Lobster	*Ise-ebi*
Mackerel	*Saba*
Mantis shrimp	*Shako*
Octopus	*Tako*
Oyster	*Kaki*
Pacific saury	*Samma*
Pike, Barracuda	*Kamasu*
Prawn	*Kuruma ebi*
Pufferfish (see P.74)	*Fugu*
Rainbow trout	*Nigimasu*
River trout	*Masu*
Salmon	*Sa-ke*

Salmon roe	*Ikura*
Sardine, Anchovy	*Iwashi*
Scallop	*Hotategai*
Scallop centers	*Kaibashira*
Sea bass	*Suzuki*
Sea bream	*Tai*
Sea cucumber	*Namako*
Sea eel	*Anago, Hamo*
Sea urchin	*Uni*
Shrimp	*Ebi*
Smelt	*Shishamo*
Spanish mackerel	*Sawara*
Squid, Cuttlefish	*Ika*
Sweet smelt	*Ayu*
Swordfish	*Mekajiki*
Turbot, Flatfish	*Karei*
Whitefish	*Shira-uo*
Yellowtail	*Buri, Hamachi*

VEGETABLES

Asparagus	*Asuparagasu*
Bamboo shoots	*Takenoko*
Bean sprouts	*Moyashi*
Beets	*Biitsu*
Brussel sprouts	*Mekyabetsu*
Butterbur stalk	*Fuki*
Cabbage	*Kyabetsu*
Carrots	*Ninjin*
Celery	*Serori*
Champignon	*Masshuruumu*
Chestnuts	*Kuri*
Chinese cabbage	*Hakusai*
Chrysanthemum leaves	*Shungiku*
Corn	*Toomorokoshi*
Cucumber	*Kyuri*
Devil's tongue root	*Konnyaku, Shirataki*

Eggplant	*Nasu*
Gingko nuts	*Ginnan*
Leek	*Negi*
Lemon-mint leaf	*Shiso*
Lettuce	*Retasu*
Lotus root	*Renkon*
Mountain vegetables	*Sansai*
Mushrooms	*Kinoko*
Mushrooms, oriental	*Shiitake*
Mushrooms, pine	*Matsutake*
Mushrooms, shoestring	*Enoki dake*
Mushrooms, slender	*Shimeji*
Mushrooms, tiny slippery	*Nameko*
Navy beans	*Shiro ingen*
Noodles	*Men*
Noodles, buckwheat	*Soba*
Noodles, egg Chinese	*Raamen, Yakisoba*
Noodles, flat wheat	*Kishimen*
Noodles, thin	*Somen, Hiyamugi*
Noodles, thick wheat	*Udon*
Onion	*Tamanegi*
Peas, green	*Gurin piisu*
Peas, snow	*Saya endo*
Peppers, green small	*Piiman, Shishito*
Peppers, red	*Aka piiman*
Potato	*Jagaimo*
Potato, sweet	*Satsumaimo*
Radish, Japanese	*Daikon*
Rice	*Kome, Gohan*
Rice dishes	*Kamameshi, Domburi*
Seaweed	*Wakame, Kombu*
Soybean curd	*Tofu*
Soybeans, green	*Edamame*
Spinach	*Horenso*
Squash, Pumpkin	*Kabocha*

Stringbeans	*Ingen, Saya ingen*
Taro	*Sato imo*
Tomato	*Tomato*
Trefoil, Marsh parsley	*Mitsuba*
Turnip	*Kabu*
Vegetables	*Yasai*
Water chestnuts	*Kuwai*
Yam	*Yama imo*

FRUITS

Apple	*Ringo*
Apricot	*Anzu*
Banana	*Banana*
Cherries	*Sakurambo*
Figs	*Ichi jiku*
Fruit	*Kudamono*
Grapefruit	*Gureepu furuutsu*
Grapes	*Budo*
Lemon	*Remon*
Musk melon	*Meron*
Oranges, mandarin	*Mikan*
Oranges, western	*Orenji*
Pear, Japanese	*Nashi*
Pear, western	*Yo-nashi*
Pineapple	*Painappuru*
Plum, Japanese	*Sumomo*
Plum, western	*Seiyo sumomo*
Peach	*Momo*
Strawberries	*Ichigo*
Watermelon	*Suika*

SAUCES AND SPICES

Aginomoto	*Kagaku Choomiryo*
Bean paste (esp. for *Konnyaku*)	*Miso*

Cheese	*Chiizu*
Cream	*Kuriimu*
Fish shavings	*Katsuo bushi*
Garlic	*Nin-niku*
Ginger	*Shooga*
Green Horseradish (for *Sushi*)	*Wasabi*
Green seaweed flakes	*Ao-nori*
Hot mustard (esp. for *Oden*)	*Karashi*
Lemon-mint leaf	*Shiso*
Okonomiyaki sauce	*Sosu*
Pepper (for *Unagi*)	*Sansho*
Pepper, ground black	*Kosho*
Raw egg (for *Sukiyaki*)	*Nama tamago*
Salad dressing	*Sarada doressingu*
Salt	*Shio*
Seaweed sheets, crisp	*Nori*
Sesame seeds	*Goma*
Shabu-shabu citrus dip	*Ponzu*
Shabu-shabu sesame dip	*Goma dare*
Sour plum	*Umeboshi*
Soy sauce	*Shoyu*
Sweet sake	*Mirin*
Tempura sauce	*Tentsuyu*
Tonkatsu sauce	*Sosu*
Vinegar	*Su*
Walnuts	*Kurumi*
Worcestershire sauce	*Sosu*

●INDEX TO RESTAURANT NAMES

All restaurants in this guide are listed below in alphabetical order to make it easy to find a restaurant you once visited or have simply heard about. The numbers listed below indicate which map to use and what restaurant numbers to look for. Stars indicate highly recommended restaurants. **Example**, ☆ 3–5 means: use map 3 and look on it for restaurant No. 5 which is a highly recommended restaurant.

● ABOUT THE AUTHORS

Russell Marcus' first taste of real Japanese cuisine was during business luncheons and dinners with Japanese trading companies in 1969. The food made such a positive impression on him, among other things, that he married a Japanese cook in 1974. Years later after he moved to Japan in 1978, while taking some overseas guests out to dinner, Russ became aware of the need for a book which would permit diners to quickly find good restaurants in any part of the Tokyo metropolis and to order from Japanese menus without a translator. His computer and software talents were responsible for organizing and keeping tabs on over 1500 restaurants which were surveyed during the preparation of this Guide. Currently, he resides in Tokyo with his wife and two bilingual children.

Jack Plimpton's interest in Japanese food began as a regular guest taster on a Sendai television variety show featuring Japanese chefs. At that time he was improving his Harvard acquired fluency in the Japanese language under a Rotary scholarship at Tohoku University in Sendai. Jack continued eating his way around Japan as a journalist for the Asahi Evening News and Shukan Sankei, writing articles on Japanese food and other topics in both English and Japanese. His ability as a simultaneous interpreter was invaluable in interviewing chefs and researching Japanese source materials in the preparation of this Guide. Jack has freelanced for many newspapers, including the National Enquirer, and has been the Tokyo Correspondent for Advertising Age and Asiaweek. Now a resident of Northern California, Jack recently graduated from the Stanford Graduate School of Business.

● FOR READER LETTERS

We, the authors, are very interested to hear from any-one regarding your experiences in using this Guide or about your dining interests. To help us in responding to your letters, we request you to return this page or a copy of it with your letter, with the following informa-tion.

Name:_____

Address:_____

_____

Occupation and title:_____

Where I heard of this Guide:_____

Subject of my letter:

☐ Gourmet tales and discoveries

☐ Gourmet events in Japan

☐ Gourmet tours for parties and organizations

☐ Newsletters, articles and future publications

☐ New restaurant openings

☐ Quantity discounts for bulk orders

☐ Suggestions for the next edition

☐ _____

To get in touch with the authors, simply write to them in English at the following address:

> Japanese Gourmet Dining Association
> c/o Shufunotomo Co., Ltd.
> 6, Kanda Surugadai 1-chome
> Chiyoda-ku, Tokyo
> Japan 101

Guidebooks from Shufunotomo

Eating Cheap in Japan
by Kimiko Nagasawa & Camy Condon

The *gaijin* gourmet's guide to ordering in non-tourist restaurants. Dishes peculiar to Japan are presented alphabetically in color.

Kites, Crackers and Craftsmen
by Kimiko Nagasawa & Camy Condon

An invitation to the most representative and traditional Japanese shops in Tokyo with addresses, maps, histories and shopping hints.

A Parents' Guide to Tokyo
by Nancy Hartzenbusch & Alice Shabecoff

A complete guide to parks, zoos, aquariums, museums, shopping, tours, lessons, and so on.

A Guide to the Gardens of Kyoto
by Marc Treib & Ron Herman

Designed for the layman as well as the professional, this concise guide provides both practical information and theoretical insights into the design of the Japanese garden.

Earth 'n' Fire
by Amaury Saint-Gilles

This book introduces many potteries and kilns throughout Japan giving a glimpse of what to expect and where to find each without too much trouble.

Japanese Prints Today
by Margaret K. Johnson & Dale K. Hilton

Twenty-two Japanese printmakers share their ideas and imaginative approaches to woodblock, intaglio, lithography and stencil processes. Guide to Tokyo galleries included.

Japanese Illustrated
by Edward A. Schwarz & Reiko Ezawa

Meeting Japan through her language. More than 400 Japanese things are explained with cartoons and photographs.